A Machine Learning Approach to Phishing Detection and Defense

A Machine Learning Approach to Phishing Detection and Defense

Oluwatobi Ayodeji Akanbi
Iraj Sadegh Amiri
Elahe Fazeldehkordi

AMSTERDAM • BOSTON • HEIDELBERG
LONDON • NEW YORK • OXFORD • PARIS
SAN DIEGO • SAN FRANCISCO
SINGAPORE • SYDNEY • TOKYO

Syngress is an Imprint of Elsevier

Acquiring Editor: Chris Katsaropoulos
Editorial Project Manager: Benjamin Rearick
Project Manager: Preethy Simon

Syngress is an imprint of Elsevier
225 Wyman Street, Waltham, MA 02451, USA

Library of Congress Cataloging-in-Publication Data
A catalog record for this book is available from the Library of Congress

British Library Cataloguing-in-Publication Data
A catalogue record for this book is available from the British Library

ISBN: 978-0-12-802927-5

For information on all Syngress publications
visit our website at store.elsevier.com/Syngress

CONTENTS

ABSTRACT

Phishing is a kind of cyber-attack in which perpetrators use spoofed emails and fraudulent web sites to lure unsuspecting online users into giving up personal information. This project looks at the phishing problem holistically by examining various research works and their countermeasures, and how to increase detection. It composes of three studies. In the first study, focus was on dataset gathering, pre-processing, features extraction and dataset division in order to make the dataset suitable for the classification process. In the second study, focus was on metric evaluation of a set of classifiers (C4.5, SVM, KNN and LR) using the accuracy, precision, recall and f-measure metrics. The output of the individual classifier study is used to choose the best performed individual classifier. The final study is divided into two parts; the first part focus on the increasing detection rate in phishing website algorithm by choosing a suitable design for classifier ensemble and also choosing the best ensemble classifier which will then be in comparison with the best individual classifier. The second part focused on choosing the better of the two studies. The resulting outcome of the study shows that the individual classifier method performed better with an accuracy of 99.37% while the chosen ensemble had an accuracy of 99.31%. This result can be attributed to the small size of dataset used as it was shown in past researches that K-NN performs better with a decreasing size of dataset while classifiers like SVM and C4.5 performs better with increasing size of dataset.

LIST OF TABLES

LIST OF FIGURES

LIST OF ABBREVIATION

ANN	Artificial Neural Network
APWG	Anti-Phishing Work Group
BART	Bayesian Additive Regression Trees
C4.5	Decision Tree
CA	Certificate Authority
DNS	Domain Name System
DR	Detection Rate
ENS	Ensemble
FAR	False Alarm Rate
FP	False Positive
FN	False Negative
FNR	False Negative Rate
FPR	False Positive Rate
HTML	Hyper Text Markup Language
HTTP	Hyper Text Transfer Protocol
HTTPS	Hyper Text Transfer Protocol Secure
IP	Internet Protocol
K-NN	K-Nearest Neighbor
LR	Linear Regression
MLP	Multi Layer Perceptron
NB	Naïve Bayesian
Pred.	Prediction
ROC	Receiver Operating Characteristic
SQL	Structured Query Language
SSL	Secure Socket Layer
SVM	Support Vector Machine
TP	True Positive
TPR	True Positive Rate
TN	True Negative
TTL	Time to Live
URL	Uniform Resource Locator
URI	Uniform Resource Identifier

CHAPTER 1

Introduction

1.1 INTRODUCTION

Cybercrime refers to crimes that target computer or network such that the computers may or may not have been fully instrumental to the commission of the crime (Martin et al., 2011). Computer crimes consist of a broad range of potentially criminal activities. However, it can be categorized into either of two parts (Martin et al., 2011):

1. Crimes that directly target computers, networks, or devices, and
2. Crimes aided by computers, networks, or devices, the main aim of which is not targeted at computer network or device.

Some examples of cybercrimes include spam, cyber terrorism, fraud, and phishing.

Phishing is an online identity theft in which an attacker uses fraudulent e-mails and bogus website in order to trick gullible customers into disclosing confidential information such as bank account information, website login information, and so forth. (Topkara et al., 2005). Phishing is an indicative type of illegal fraudulent attempt in online electronic communication. Phishing is a form of internet scam in which an attacker makes use of an email or website to illegally obtain private (Martin et al., 2011). It is a semantic attack which aims at harming the user rather than the computer. In general, phishing is a relatively new internet crime. The ease of cloning a legitimate bank website to convince unsuspecting users has made phishing difficult to curtail. Mostly, an email with a redirecting website link is sent to the user to update confidential information such as credit card, website login information, and bank account information that belongs to the licit. As explained by Aburrous et al. (2008), the complexity of understanding and analyzing phishing website is as a result of its involvement with technical problems and social. The main effect of phishing website is in the abuse of information through the compromise of user data that may harm victims in form of financial losses or valuables. Phishing in comparison to other forms of internet threat such as hacking and virus is a fast growing internet crime. In the broad usage of internet as a major form of communication, phishing can be implemented in different ways such as follows (Alnajim and Munro, 2009):

1. Email-to-email: when someone receives an email requesting sensitive information to be sent to the sender.
2. Email-to-website: when someone receives an email embedded with phishing web address.
3. Website-to-website: when someone clicks on phishing website through a search engine or an online advert.
4. Browser-to-website: when someone misspelled a legitimate web address on a browser and then referred to a phishing website that has a semantic similarity to the legitimate web address.

Different types of anti-phishing measures are being used to prevent phishing, such as, Anti-Phishing Working Group is an industry group, which formulates phishing reports from different online incident resources and makes it available to its paying members (RSA, 2006). Meanwhile, anti-phishing measures have been implemented as additional extension or toolbars for browsers, as features embedded in browsers, and as part of website login operation. Many of these toolbars have been used in the detection of phishing. Garera et al. (2007) proposed SpoofGuard which warns users of phishing website user (Chou et al., 2004). This tool makes use of URL, images, domain name, and link to evaluate the spoof likelihood.

Lucent Personalized Web Assistant (LPWA) is a tool that guards against identity theft to protect user's personal information (Gabber et al., 1999, Kristol et al., 1998). It uses a function to define user variables such as email address, username, and password for each server visited by the user. Ross et al. (2005), proposed a similar approach in PwdHash.

Dhamija and Tygar (2005b) propose Dynamic Security Skins, which is another type of browser-based anti-phishing. This solution was implemented on the basis of their previous work on Human Interactive Proofs (Dhamija and Tygar, 2005a), which employs distinguishing features between legitimate and spoofed websites by human. Dynamic Security Skins ensures identity verification of a remote server by humans, but is hard to spoof by attackers (Dhamija and Tygar, 2005b). Furthermore, the tool uses a client-side password on the browser window with a secure remote password protocol (SRP) for verification-based authentication protocol. In addition, an image which is shared as a secret between the browser and the user ensures better security against spoofing. This secured image is either chosen by the user or as a result of random assignment and also, during each transaction, the image is being regenerated by the server and used in creating the browser skin. As a verification measure for the server, the user has to visually verify if the authenticity of the image. In exceptional cases when the user logs in from an untrusted computer, the tool will not be able to guarantee security Furthermore, it does not guard against malware and trusts the browser's security during the SRP authentication.

Herzberg and Gbara (2004) introduced TrustBar which is a third-party certification solution against phishing. The authors proposed creating a Trusted Credentials Area (TCA). The TCA controls a significant area, located at the top of every browser window, and large enough to contain highly visible logos and other graphical icons for credentials identifying a legitimate page. Although their solution does not rely on complex security factors, it does not prevent against spoofing attacks. Specifically, since the logos of websites do not change, they can be used by an attacker to create a look alike TCA in an untrusted web page.

Due to the ever increasing phishing websites springing up by the day, it is becoming increasingly difficult to track and block them as attackers are coming up with innovative methods every day to entice unsuspecting users into divulging their personal information (Garera et al., 2007).

1.2 PROBLEM BACKGROUND

As a new type of cyber security threat, phishing websites appear frequently in recent years, which have led to great harm in online financial services and data security (Zhuang et al., 2012). It has been projected that the vulnerability of most web servers have led to the evolution of most phishing websites such that the weakness in the web server is exploited by phishers to host counterfeiting website without the knowledge of the owner. It is also possible that the phisher hosts a new web server independent of any legitimate web server for phishing activities. Zhang et al. (2012) claimed that the method used in carrying out phishing can be different across regions. Furthermore, he also deduced that the phishers in America and China region have different approaches that he categorized into two on the basis of region:

1. The Chinese phishers prefer to register a new domain to deploy the phishing website.
2. The American phishers would rather deploy the phishing website using a hacked website.

Most researchers have worked on increasing the accuracy of website phishing detection through multiple techniques. Several classifiers such as Linear Regression, K-Nearest Neighbor, C5.0, Naïve Bayes, Support Vector Machine (SVM), and Artificial Neural Network among others have been used to train datasets in identifying phishing websites. These classifiers can be classified into two techniques: either probabilistic or machine learning. Based on these algorithms, several problems regarding phishing website detection have been solved by different researchers. Some of these algorithms were evaluated using four metrics, precision, recall, F1-Score, and accuracy.

Some studies have applied K-Nearest Neighbour (KNN) for phishing website classification. KNN classifier is a nonparametric classification algorithm. One of the characteristic of this classifier is that it generalizes whenever it is required to classify an instance. This has the effect of ensuring that no information is lost as can happen with the other eager learning techniques (Toolan and Carthy 2009). In addition, previous researches have shown that KNN can achieve accurate results, and sometimes more accurate than those of the symbolic classifiers. It was shown in a study carried out by Kim and Huh (2011) that KNN classifier achieved 99% detection rate. This result was better than the one obtained from LDA, Naïve Bayesian (NB), and Support Vector Machine (SVM). Also, since the performance of KNN is primarily determined by the choice of K, they tried to find the best K by varying it from 1 to 5; and found that KNN performs best when K = 1. This as well, helped in the high accuracy of KNN compared to other classifiers ensemble.

Meanwhile, Artificial Neural Network (ANN) is another popular machine learning technique. It consists of a collection of processing elements that are highly interconnected and transform a set of inputs to a set of desired outputs. The major disadvantage is in the time it takes for parameter selection and network learning. On the other hand, previous researches have shown that ANN can achieve very accurate results compared to other learning classification techniques. In a research carried out by Basnet et al. (2008), it was shown that Artificial Neural Network achieved an accuracy of 97.99%.

Based on related research (Aburrous et al., 2008; Alnajim and Munro, 2009; Kim and Huh, 2011; Miyamoto et al., 2007; Topkara et al., 2005; Zhang et al., 2012), successful rates have been achieved on detection accuracy using different learning algorithm but still website phishing detection is very much open for research because the rate at which phishing websites are deployed and the method used is faster than the solutions proposed by researchers. Generally, most of the recent studies were conducted on a small experimental data set, the robustness and effectiveness of these algorithms on real large-scale data sets cannot be guaranteed; furthermore, the number of phishing sites grows very fast, how to identify phishing websites from mass of legitimate websites in real time must also be addressed. As proposed by Miyamoto et al. (2007), in order to deal with the ever increasing phishing attacks, developing intelligent anti-phishing algorithms is paramount. Fundamentally, the detection algorithms are grouped into two distinct methods, which are URL filtering and URL whitelist-based detection method (Miyamoto et al., 2005).

The variation in the performance of different algorithms used in website phishing detection has led to ensemble. Classifier ensemble is a method of using various classifiers in enhancing analytical performance of individual component algorithm (Rokach, 2010). A study carried out by Toolan and Carthy (2009) showed an approach to categorizing phishing emails and nonphishing emails by using an algorithm known to achieve very high precision with other classifiers in ensemble (K-Nearest Neighbour, Support Vector Machine, Naïve Bayes, and Linear Regression) that achieve high recall. A success rate of more than 99% was obtained during their experiment. As a starting point, the work of Toolan and Carthy will be used as a baseline for this research since their success rate using ensemble method in email phishing detection is very impressive. As such, it is possible to improve performance of website phishing detection using ensemble method.

1.3 PROBLEM STATEMENT

Phishing detection techniques do suffer low detection accuracy and high false alarm especially when novel phishing approaches are introduced. Besides, the most common technique used, blacklist-based method is inefficient in responding to emanating phishing attacks since registering new domain has become easier, no comprehensive blacklist can ensure a perfect up-to-date database. Furthermore, page content inspection has been used by some strategies to overcome the false negative problems and complement the vulnerabilities of the stale lists. Moreover, page content inspection algorithms each have different approach to phishing website detection with varying degrees of accuracy. Therefore, ensemble can be seen to be a better solution as it can combine the similarity in accuracy and different error-detection rate properties in selected algorithms. Therefore, this study will address a couple of research:

1. How to process raw dataset for phishing detection?
2. How to increase detection rate in phishing websites algorithms?
3. How to reduce false negative rate in phishing websites algorithm?
4. What are the best compositions of classifiers that can give a good detection rate of phishing website?

1.4 PURPOSE OF STUDY

In this research, performance of individual classifiers as well as the ensemble of classifiers that utilizes different learning paradigms and voting scheme will be compared in terms of detection accuracy and false negative. At the end of this comparison, the algorithm that shows better performance in terms of detection accuracy and low false negative rate will be highlighted.

1.5 PROJECT OBJECTIVES

There are four objectives for this project. They are:

1. To carry out dataset processing and feature extraction.
2. To evaluate individual classifiers performance in varying dataset.
3. To determine the best design ensemble and select the best ensemble classifier.

4. To compare the result obtained at the end of the ensemble with the results obtained from individual algorithm.

1.6 SCOPE OF STUDY

The scopes of this research are as follow:

1. The phishing dataset is obtained from phishtank (www.phishtank.com) whereas the legitimate website is obtained manually using Google webcrawlers.
2. First, the dataset is divided into three sets which are then used to train and test the algorithms; Decision Tree (C4.5), Support Vector Machine (SVM), Linear Regression (LR), and K-Nearest Neighbor KNN.
3. The performance metrics of the reference algorithms based on precision, recall, f1-score and accuracy of the three algorithms are compared.
4. The website features are categorized based on five criteria: URL and Domain Identity, Security and Encryption, Source Code and Java Script, Page Style and Content and Web Address
5. Experimental implementation of this project is done using rapidminer.

1.7 THE SIGNIFICANCE OF STUDY

Nowadays, there is an increasing need to detect phishing websites due to the adverse effect they can have on their victims. Lots of work has been done on website phishing detection using several techniques to achieve the same goal. This study evaluates the performance of ensemble method and individual algorithms: C5.0, SVM, and LR algorithms as regards to detection accuracy and false alarms by studying each of them individually and in ensemble mode and investigate to show which is more suitable to be used in phishing detection.

1.8 ORGANIZATION OF REPORT

The book consists of six chapters. Chapter 1 describes the introduction, background of the study, research objectives and questions, the scope of the study and its primary objectives. Chapter 2 reviews available and related literature on website phishing detection. Chapter 3 describes the study methodology along with the appropriate framework for the study. Chapter 4 describes the dataset collection, preprocessing technique used, feature extraction, and dataset division. Chapter 5 discusses the implementation, result and analysis based on research framework. Finally, Chapter 6 concludes the book with a closing remark, recap of objectives, contribution, and future work.

CHAPTER 2

Literature Review

2.1 INTRODUCTION

This chapter primarily reviews the available literature in the field under study. Accordingly, it will account for the definitions of concepts and issues that affect website phishing detection using different techniques and approaches. The first part of this chapter will describe phishing and its various classifications. The second part of this chapter will deal with existing techniques and approaches that are related to detecting phishing websites. The third part discusses three types of classifier designs and their impact on website phishing detection. The fourth and the final part of this chapter reviews earlier works related to phishing detection in websites.

2.2 PHISHING

The definition of phishing in this context is essentially not so fixed but can be seen like an indisputable fact that changes with respect to the way in which phishing is carried out. More particularly, the use of email and website are the two methods of phishing. Although there are some differences between this two methods but they both share their goals in common.

In addition, phishing can be said to be an online attack used by perpetrators in committing fraud through social engineering schemes via instant messages, emails, or online advertisement to lure users to phishing websites similar to a legitimate website for gaining confidential information about the victim such as password, financial account, personal identification, and financial account numbers, which can then be used for illegal profit (Liu et al., 2010). As explained by Abbasi and Chen (2009b), phishing websites can be divided into two common types, namely; spoof and concocted websites. Spoof sites are sham replica of existing commercial websites (Dhamija et al., 2006, Dinev, 2006).

Commonly spoofed websites include eBay, PayPal, various banking and escrow service providers (Abbasi and Chen, 2009a), and e-tailers. Spoof websites attempt to steal unsuspecting users' identities; account logins, personal information, credit card numbers, and so forth. (Dinev, 2006). Online phish repositories such as PhishTank maintain URLs for millions of verified spoof websites used in phishing attacks intended to mimic thousands of legitimate entities. Fictitious websites mislead users by attempting to give the impression of unique, legitimate commercial entities such as investment banks, escrow services, shipping companies, and online pharmacies (Abbasi and Chen, 2009b; Abbasi et al., 2012; Abbasi et al., 2010). The aim of fictitious websites is failure-to-ship scam; swindling customers' of their money without keeping to their own end of the bargain (Chua and Wareham, 2004). Both spoof and concocted websites are also commonly used to propagate malware and viruses (Willis, 2009).

In a personal fraud survey carried out by Jamieson et al. (2012) indicate the percentage of phishing in identity crime reclassification using publicly available data by Australia Bureau of Statistic (ABS) as a case study. The outcome showed that phishing constitutes a fraction of 0.4% which corresponded to 57,800 victims. Figures 2.1 and 2.2 represent the survey information.

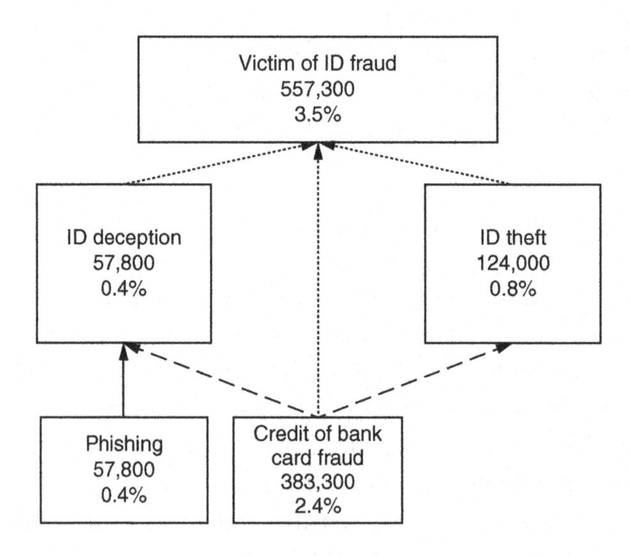

Fig. 2.1. Identity crime reclassification of ABS (personal crime survey 2008). (Jamieson et al., 2012)

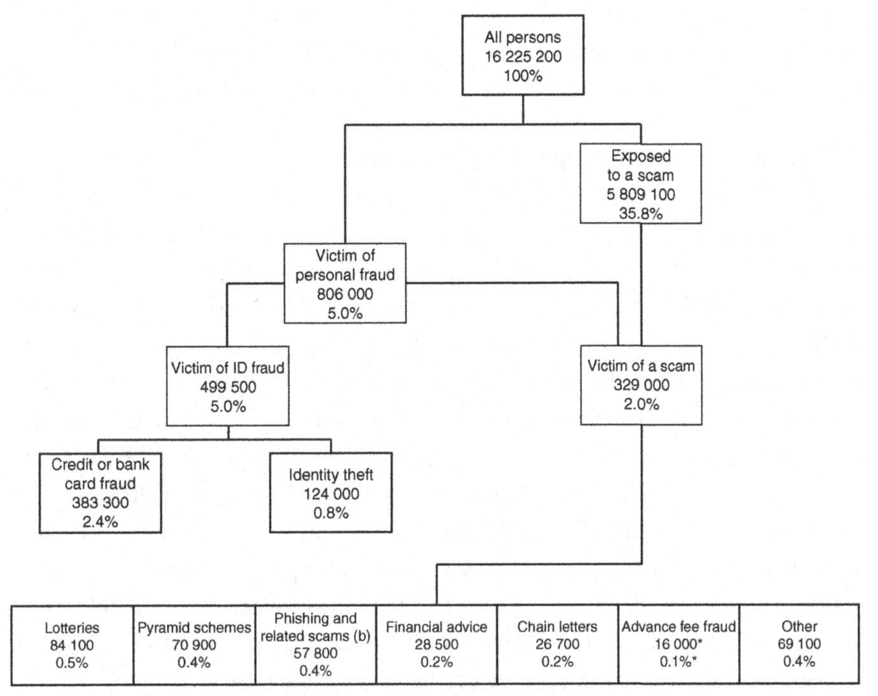

* Estimate has a relative standard error of 25% to 50% and should be used with caution.
(a) People who expenenced personal frauds could have experienced more than one incident. The components when added may therefore be larger than the total.
(b) Also includes other methods, such as by phone, to obtain a person's bank account of personal details. For more information, see the glossary.

Fig. 2.2. Experience of selected personal frauds. (Jamieson et al., 2012)

2.3 EXISTING ANTI-PHISHING APPROACHES

In a study review published by Anti-Phishing Working Group (APWG), there were at least 67, 677 phishing attacks in the last 6 months of 2010 (A.P.W.G, 2010). A lot of research has been done on anti-phishing in designing various anti-phishing approaches. Afroz and Greenstadt (2009), categorized the current phishing detection into three main types: (1) non-content-based approaches that do not make use of site content to classify it as authentic or phishing, (2) content-based approaches that make use of site contents to catch phishing, and (3) visual similarity-based approaches that uses visual similarity with known sites to recognize phishing. These approaches are discussed in subsequent sections.

Other anti-phishing approaches include detecting phishing emails (Fette et al., 2007) (rather than sites) and educating users about phishing attacks and human detection methods (Kumaraguru et al., 2007).

2.3.1 Non-Content-Based Approaches

In a study carried out by Afroz and Greenstadt (2009), it was claimed that non-content-based approaches include URL and host information based classification of phishing sites, blacklisting, and whitelisting methods. In URL-based schemes, URLs are classified on the basis of both lexical and host features. Lexical features describe lexical patterns of malicious URLs. These include features such as length of the URL, the number of dots, special characters it contains. Host features of the URL include properties of IP address, the owner of the site, DNS properties such as TTL, and geographical location (Ma et al., 2009). Using these features, a matrix is built and run through multiple classification algorithms. In real-time processing trials, this approach has success rates between 95% and 99%. According toAfroz and Greenstadt (2009), they used lexical features of URL along with site contents and image analysis to improve performance and reduce false positive cases.

In blacklisting approaches, reports made by users or companies are used to detect phishing websites which are stored in a database. Perhaps the use of this approach by commercial toolbars such as Netcraft, Internet explorer 7, CallingID Toolbar, EarthLink Toolbar, Cloudmark Anti-Fraud Toolbar, GeoTrust TrustWatch Toolbar, Netscape Browser 8.1 has made it very popular amongst other anti-phishing approaches (Afroz and Greenstadt, 2009). Nonetheless, as most phishing sites are temporary and often times exist for less than 20 hours (Moore and Clayton, 2007), or change URLs frequently (fast-flux), the URL blacklisting approach fails to identify majority of phishing incidents. Furthermore, a blacklisting approach will fail to detect an attack that is aim at a specific user (spear-phishing), especially those that aim profitable but not extensively used sites such as small brokerages, company intranets, and so forth (Afroz and Greenstadt, 2009).

Whitelisting approaches seek to identify known good sites (Chua and Wareham, 2004, Close, 2009; Herzberg and Jbara, 2008), but a user must remember to inspect the interface whenever he visits any site. Some whitelisting approaches use server-side validation to add additional authentication metrics (beyond SSL) to client browsers as a proof of its benign nature, For example, dynamic security skins (Kumaraguru et al., 2007), TrustBar (Herzberg and Gbara, 2004), SRD (Synchronized Random Dynamic Boundaries) (Ye et al., 2005).

2.3.2 Content-Based Approaches

According to content-based approach, phishing attacks are detected by investigating site contents. Features used in this approach comprise of password fields, spelling errors, source of the images, links, embedded links, and so forth alongside URL and host-based features. SpoofGuard (Chou et al., 2004) and CANTINA (Zhang et al., 2007) are two examples of content-based approach. In addition, Google's anti-phishing filter detects phishing and malware by examining page URL, page rank, WHOIS information and contents of a page including HTML, javascript, images, iframe, and so forth (Whittaker et al., 2010). The classifier is frequently retrained with new phishing sites to learn new trends in phishing. This classifier has high accuracy but is presently implemented offline as it takes 76 seconds on average to detect phishing. Some researchers studied fingerprinting and fuzzy logic-based approaches that use a series of hashes of websites to identify phishing sites (Aburrous et al., 2008; Zdziarski et al., 2006). Furthermore, experimentation of Afroz and Greenstadt (2009) with a fuzzy hashing-based approach suggested that this approach can identify present attacks, only that it can be easily evaded by restructuring HTML elements without changing the appearance of the site.

Furthermore, GoldPhish (Dunlop et al., 2010) tool implements this approach and uses Google as its search engine. This tool gives higher rank to well-established websites. It has been observed that phishing web pages are operational only for short period of time and as a result will acquire low rank during internet query making it a basis for content-based anti-phishing approach (Dunlop et al., 2010). The design approach can be summarized into three key steps. (1) an image capture of the current website in the user's web browser (2) the conversion of captured image into computer readable text using optical character recognition, and (3) input the converted text into a search engine to retrieve results and evaluate the page rank. One of the benefits of this tool is that, it does not result in false positive and provides zero-day protection against zero-day phishing attack (Dunlop et al., 2010). The drawback of GoldPhish is the time it takes in the rendering of a webpage. It is also susceptible to Google's PageRank algorithm and Google's search service attacks (Dunlop et al., 2010).

2.3.3 Visual Similarity-Based Approach

Chen et al. (2009) used screenshot of web pages to identify phishing sites. They used Contrast Context Histogram (CCH) to describe the images of web pages and k-mean algorithm to cluster nearest key points. Lastly, euclidean distance between two descriptors is used to obtain similarity between two sites. Their approach attained an accuracy of 95–99% with 0.1% false positive. Chen et al. (2009) claimed that screenshot analysis lack efficiency in proper detection of online phishing.

Fu et al. (2006) utilized Earth Mover's Distance (EMD) to associate low-resolution screen capture of a web page. Images of web pages are denoted through the aid of image pixel color (alpha, red, green, and blue) and the centroid of its position distribution in the image. They used machine learning to select different threshold appropriate for different web pages.

Matthew Dunlop investigated the use of optical character recognition to convert screenshot of websites to text and then utilized Google PageRank to identify legitimate and phishing sites (Dunlop et al., 2010).

In addition, visual similarity-based approaches includes visual similarity assessment by means of layout and style similarity (Liu et al., 2006) and iTrustPage (Ronda et al., 2008) that uses Google search and user judgment to identify visually similar pages.

2.3.4 Character-Based Approach

Many times phishers try to steal information of users by convincing them to click on the hyperlink that they embed into phishing email. A hyperlink has a structure as follows. <ahref = "URI"> Anchor text <\a> (Chen and Guo, 2006) where "URI" (universal resource identifiers) gives the actual link where the user will be directed and "Anchor text" is the text that will be displayed in user's web browser and denotes the visual link.

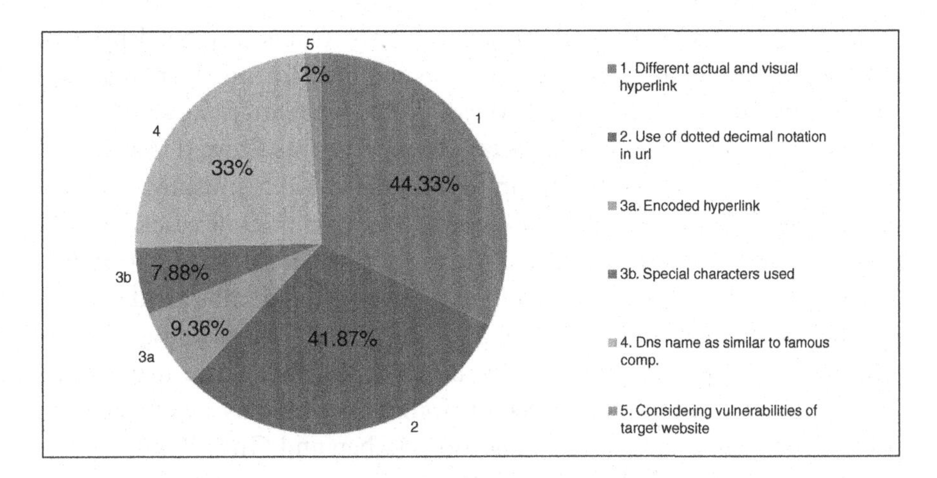

Fig. 2.3. Linkguard analysis in various classified hyperlink. (Chen and Guo, 2006)

Character-based anti-phishing technique utilizes characteristics of hyperlink in order to identify phishing links. Linkguard (Chen and Guo, 2006) is a tool that implements this technique. After analyzing many phishing websites, the hyperlinks can be classified into various categories as shown in Figure 2.3. For detection of phishing sites LinkGuard, the DNS names from the actual and the visual links will be initially extracted and then matches the actual and visual DNS names, if these names do not match, then it is phishing of category 1 and if dotted decimal IP address is directly used in actual DNS, it is then a potential phishing attack of category 2 (Chen and Guo, 2006).

If the actual link or the visual link is encoded (categories 3 and 4), then first the link is decoded and then analyzed. When there is no destination information (dotted IP address or DNS name) in the visual link then the hyperlink is analyzed. During analysis DNS name is searched in blacklist and whitelist. If it is present in whitelist then it is sure that the link is genuine, and if link is present in blacklist then it is sure that link is phished one.

If the real DNS is not contained in either whitelist or blacklist, pattern matching is done. During pattern matching, first the sender email address is extracted and then it is searched in seed set where a list of address is maintained that are manually visited by the user. Similarity assesses the maximum likelihood of actual DNS and the DNS names in seed set. The similarity index between two strings is defined by calculating the minimal number of changes required to transform a string to the other string. Advantage – it can not only identify known attacks but also is effective to zero-day attacks. Experiments showed that LinkGuard, is capable of detecting up to 96% of zero-day phishing attacks in real time (Chen and Guo, 2006). For phishing attacks of category 1, it is certain that there are no false positives or false negatives. LinkGuard handles categories 3 and 4 correctly since the encoded links are decoded first before further analysis (Chen and Guo, 2006). Disadvantage – For category 2, LinkGuard may result in false positives, since using dotted decimal IP addresses in place of domain names may be considered necessary in some exceptional conditions (Chen and Guo, 2006).

2.4 EXISTING TECHNIQUES

Phishing attacks have mislead a lot of users by impersonating legitimate websites and stealing private information and/or financial data (Afroz and Greenstadt, 2011). To protect users against phishing, various anti-phishing techniques have been proposed that follow different strategies like client-side and server-side protection (Gaurav et al., 2012). Anti-phishing refers to the method employed in order to detect and prevent phishing attacks. Anti-phishing protects users from phishing. A lot of work has been done on anti-phishing devising various anti-phishing techniques. Some techniques work on emails, some works on attributes of websites and some on URL of the websites. Handful of these techniques emphasis on aiding clients to identify and filter various types of phishing attacks. In general, anti-phishing techniques can be grouped into subsequent four categories (Chen and Guo, 2006).

Content Filtering

In this methodology, content/email is filtered as it enters in the victim's mail box by means of machine learning methods, such as Support Vector Machines (SVM) or Bayesian Additive Regression Trees (BART) (Tout and Hafner, 2009).

Blacklisting

Blacklist is collection of recognized phishing Websites/addresses published by dependable entities like Google's and Microsoft's blacklist. It involves both a client and a server component. The client component is employed as either an email or browser plug-in that relates with a server component, which in this case is a public website that make available a list of identified phishing sites (Tout and Hafner, 2009).

Symptom-Based Prevention

Symptom-based prevention evaluates the content of each web page the user visits and spawns phishing alerts corresponding to the type and number of symptoms detected (Tout and Hafner, 2009).

Domain Binding

It is a client's browser-based techniques where sensitive information (e.g., name, password) is bind to a particular domain. It warns the user when he visits a domain to which user credential is not bind (Gaurav et al., 2012).

Also, Gaurav et al. (2012) classified phishing techniques into five categories, which are:(1) attribute-based anti-phishing technique (2) generic algorithm-based anti-phishing technique (3) identity-based anti-phishing technique (4) character-based anti-phishing approach, and (5) content-based anti-phishing approach. Subsequent sections will describe each category in details.

2.4.1 Attribute-Based Anti-Phishing Technique

Attribute-based anti-phishing strategy implements both reactive and proactive anti-phishing defenses. This technique has been implemented in PhishBouncer (Atighetchi and Pal, 2009) tool. The various checks that PhishBouncer does are shown in Figure 2.4.

The image attribution check (Atighetchi and Pal, 2009) does a comparison of images of visiting site and the sites already registered with PhishBouncer. The HTML cross-link check observes responses from nonregistered sites and amounts the number of links the page has to any of the registered sites; a high number of cross-links is suggestive of a phishing site (Atighetchi and Pal, 2009). In false info feeder (Atighetchi and Pal, 2009) check, false information is input and if that information is accepted by site then it is probable that link is phished one. The certificate suspicious check authenticates site certificates presented in the

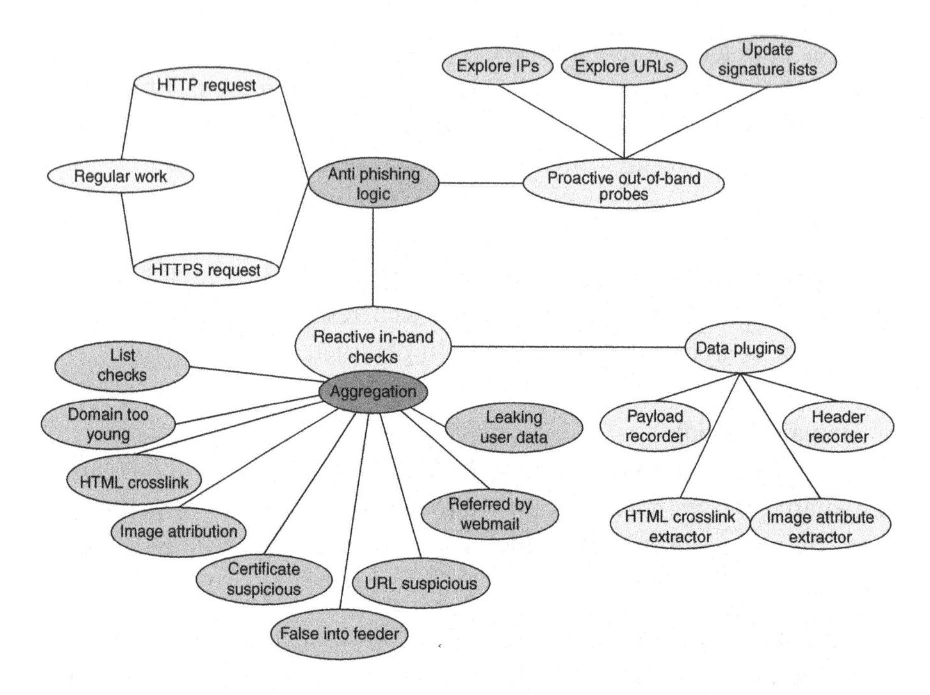

Fig. 2.4. Use case diagram. (Atighetchi and Pal, 2009)

course of SSL handshake and extends the typical usage by looking for certification authority (CA) reliability over time. URL suspicious check uses characteristics of the URL to identify phishing sites.

An advantage of this technique is that as attribute-based anti-phishing, it considers a lot of checks so it is able to detect more phished sites than other approaches. It can detect known as well as unknown attacks. The only shortcoming of this technique since it performs multiple checks to authenticate is that it may result in slow response (Gaurav et al., 2012).

2.4.2 Generic Algorithm-Based Anti-Phishing Technique

It is an approach that uses genetic algorithm for phishing web pages detection. Genetic algorithms can be used to develop simple rules for preventing phishing attacks. These rules are used to discern normal website from anomalous website. These anomalous websites denote events with probability of phishing attacks. The rules stored in the rule base are typically in the following form (Shreeram et al., 2010) (Figure 2.5):

```
    if{condition}
          then{act}
For example, a rule can be defined as:
      if {The IP adress of the URL in the received e-mail finds any
      match in the Rule set}
           Then{Phishing e-mail}(Shreeram et al., 2010)
This rule can be explained as:
       if {There exists an IP address of the URL in e-mail and it
       does not match the defined Rule Set for White List}
then{The received mail is a phishing mail}(Shreeram et al., 2010)
```

Fig. 2.5. Rules stored in rules based.

The main advantage is that it provides the feature of malicious status notification before the user reads the mail. It also provides malicious web-link detection in addition of phishing detection. The disadvantage of this technique is more to its complex algorithms; single rule for phishing detection like in case of URL is far from enough, so we need multiple rule set for only one type of URL based phishing detection. Likewise for other parameter we need to write other rule which may lead to more complex algorithm.

2.4.3 An Identity-Based Anti-Phishing Techniques

This technique follows mutual authentication methodology where both user and online entity validates each other's identity during handshake. It is a phishing detection technique that incorporates partial credentials sharing and client-filtering method to avert phishers from easily impersonating legitimate online entities. As shared authentication is followed, there would be no need for users to reenter their credentials. Hence, passwords are never exchanged between users and online entities except during the initial account setup process (Tout and Hafner, 2009).

Advantage of this technique, it provides mutual authentication for server as well as client side. Using this technique, user does not need to reveal his credential password in whole session except for the first time when the session is being initialized (Tout and Hafner, 2009).

Unfortunately, in identity-based anti-phishing, if an intruder gains access to the client computer and disables the browser plug-in then method will be compromise against phishing detection (Tout and Hafner, 2009).

2.5 DESIGN OF CLASSIFIERS

In this section, some of the existing classifier designs will be discussed. These designs include hybrid, lookup, classifier, and ensemble system.

2.5.1 Hybrid System

Hybrid systems combine classifier and lookup mechanism. The system blocks URLs on the blacklist, whereas the classifier evaluates others. Anti-phishing detection techniques are either lookup based or classifier based (Fahmy and Ghoneim, 2011). Lookup-based systems suffer from high false negatives whereas classifier systems suffer from high false positives. To better detect fraudulent websites, it was proposed by Fahmy and Ghoneim (2011), as an efficient hybrid system that is based on both lookup and a support vector machine classifier that checks features derived from websites URL, text, and linkage. In addition, PhishBlock is the first hybrid tool that uses neural networks (Figure 2.6).

Xiang and Hong (2009) proposed a hybrid phish-detection approach based on information extraction (IE) and information retrieval (IR) techniques. The identity-based component of method by Xiang and Hong (2009) identifies phishing web pages by directly discerning the contradiction between their identity and the identity they are imitating. The keywords-retrieval component employs IR algorithms in utilizing the potential of search engines to detect phish. Their system achieved a good result over a varied range of data sources with 11449 pages. It showed that both mechanisms have a low false positive rate and the stacked approach attains a true positive rate of 90.06% with a false positive rate of 1.95% (Xiang and Hong, 2009) (Figure 2.7).

In Xiang and Hong (2009) study, part of the false negatives was generated as a result of the phisher hacking into legal domains, which falsely triggered the whitelist filter. This could be improved to a certain degree by examining the web page using hybrid phish-detection system even if domain whitelist yields a match that, as a result, inadvertently raises the FP a little bit as a side effect (Xiang and Hong, 2009).

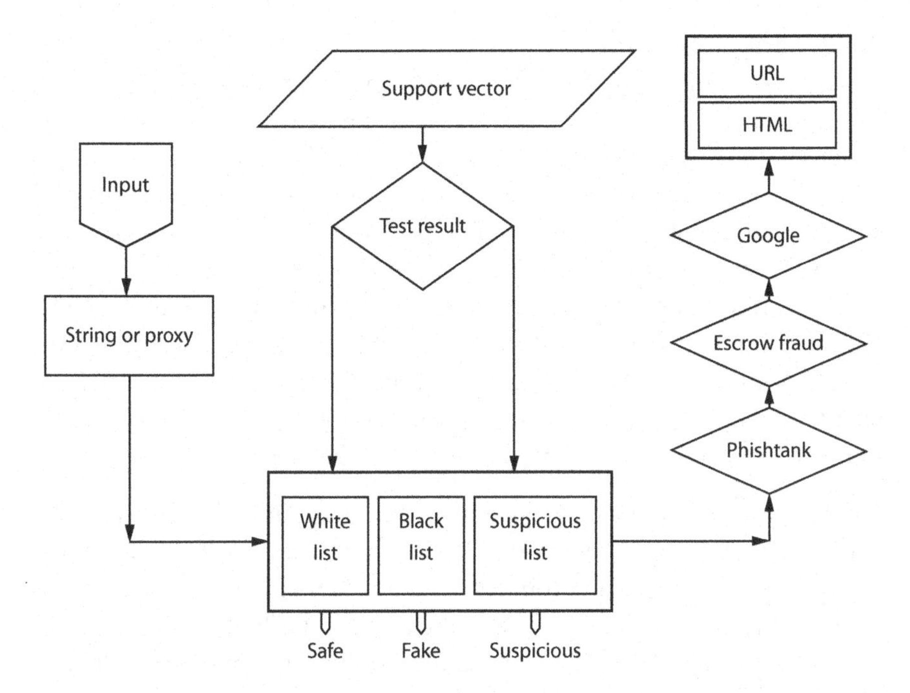

Fig. 2.6. Phishblock design. (Fahmy and Ghoneim, 2011)

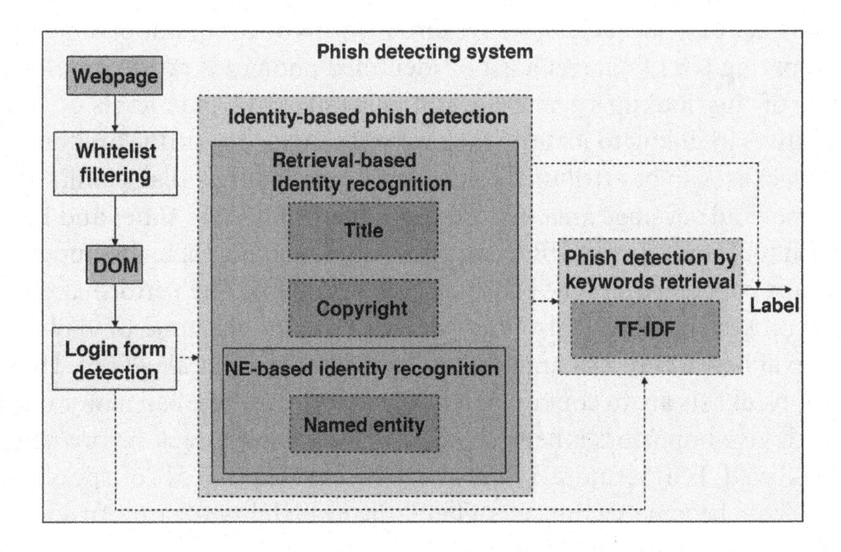

Fig. 2.7. Hybrid phish detection system architecture. (Xiang and Hong, 2009).

2.5.2 Lookup System

Lookup systems implements a client–server architecture such that the server side maintains a blacklist of known fake URLs (Li and Helenius, 2007; Zhang et al., 2006) and the client–side tool examines the blacklist and provides a warning if a website poses a threat. Lookup systems utilize collective sanctioning mechanisms akin to those in reputation ranking mechanisms (Hariharan et al., 2007). Online communities of practice and system users provide information for the blacklists. Online communities such as the Anti-Phishing Working Group and the Artists Against 4-1-9 have developed databases of known concocted and spoof websites. Lookup systems also study URLs directly reported or assessed by system users (Abbasi and Chen, 2009b).

There are several lookup systems in existence and perhaps, the most common of which is Microsoft's IE Phishing Filter, which makes use of a client-side whitelist combined with a server-side blacklist gathered from online databases and IE user reports. Similarly, Mozilla Firefox's FirePhish7 toolbar, and the EarthLink9 toolbar also maintain a blacklist of spoof URLs. Firetrust's9Sitehound system stores spoof and concocted site URLs taken from online sources such as the Artists6Against 4-1-9. A benefit of lookup9 systems is that they characteristically have high measure of accuracy as they are less likely to detect an authentic site as phony (Zhang et al., 2006). They are also simpler to work with and faster than most classifier systems in terms of computational power; comparing URLs against a list of identified phonies is rather simple. In spite of this, lookup systems are still vulnerable to higher levels of false negatives in failing to identify fake websites. Also, one of the limitations of blacklist can be attributed to the small number of available online resources and coverage area. For example, the IE Phishing Filter and FirePhish tools only amass URLs for spoof sites, making them incompetent against concocted sites (Abbasi and Chen, 2009b). The performance of lookup systems might also vary on the basis of the time of day and interval between report and evaluation time (Zhang et al., 2006). However, blacklists are to contain older fake websites rather than newer ones, which give impostors a better chance of successive attack before being blacklisted. Furthermore, Liu et al. (2006) claimed that 5% of spoof site recipients become victims in spite of the availability of a profusion of web browser integrated lookup systems.

2.5.3 Classifier System

Classifier systems are client-side tools that employ rule-based or similarity-based heuristics to content of website or domain registration information (Wu et al., 2006; Zhang et al., 2006). Several classifier systems have been created over the years to combat phishing. Spoof-Guard applies webpage7features such as image9hashes, password5encryption checks, URL4similarities, and domain registration information (Chou et al., 2004). Netcraft classifier depends on domain0registration information such as the host name, domain name, host country, and6registration date (Li and Helenius, 2007). eBay's6Account Guard tool matches the content of the6URL of interest with genuine eBay and-8PayPal sites (Zhang et al., 2006). Reasonable4Anti-Phishing (formerly SiteWatcher) uses visual7similarity evaluation based on740 body text, page style, and image8features (Liu et al., 2006). A page3qualifies as a spoof if its similarity6is above a certain7threshold when matched to a client-side4whitelist.

Abbasi and Chen (2007) claimed that classifier system can achieve better analysis for spoofed and concocted websites compared to lookup systems. Classifier systems are also pre-emptive, proficient in detecting fakes independent of blacklists. Subsequently, classifier9systems are not impacted by time of day and the interval between when a user visits a URL9and the URL's first appearance in an online9database (Zhang et al., 2006). Nevertheless4classifier systems are not without their warnings. They can take longer to classify web pages than lookup systems. They are also more prone to false positives (Zhang et al., 2006) (where positive6refers to a legitimate website). Generalizability6of classification6models over time can be another issue, especially if the fake websites constantly evolve. For6instance, the Escrow Fraud online database (http://escrow-fraud.com) has more6than 250 unique templates for6concocted sites with new ones added constantly. Effective classifier systems must employ a bevy of fraud6cues and adapt and relearn to keep pace with the sophistication6of fake websites (Levy, 2004; Liu et al., 2006). Table 2.1 shows the summary of existing6fake website detection tools.

Garera et al. (2007) discussed some of the anti-phishing tools in Table 2.2 which comprises of the following columns; tool, primary feature, and limitation.

Table 2.1 Summary of Fake Website Detection Tools

	System type			
Tool name	**Classifier**	**Lookup**	**Website type**	**Prior results (spoof sites)**
CallingID	Domain registration information	Server-side blacklist	Spoof sites	Overall: 85.9% Spoof detection: 23.0%
Cloudmark	None	Server-side blacklist	Spoof sites	Overall: 83.9% Spoof detection: 45.0%
Earthlinktoolbar	None	Server-side blacklist	Spoof sites	Overall: 90.5% Spoof detection: 68.5%
eBay Account Guard	Content similarity heuristics	Server-side blacklist	Spoof sites (primarily eBay and PayPal)	Overall: 83.2% Spoof detection: 40.0%
FirePhish	None	Server-side blacklist	Spoof sites	Overall: 89.2% Spoof detection: 61.5%
IE Phishing Filter	None	Client-side whitelist, server-side blacklist	Spoof sites	Overall: 92.0% Spoof detection: 71.5%
Netcraft	Domain registration information	Server-side blacklist	Concocted sites, spoof sites	Overall: 91.2% Spoof detection: 68.5%
Reasonable Anti-Phishing	Text and image feature similarity, stylistic feature correlation	Client-side whitelist	Spoof sites	N/A
Sitehound	None	Server-side blacklist downloaded by client	Concocted sites, spoof sites	N/A
SpoofGuard	Image hashes, password encryption, URL similarities, domain registration information	None	Concocted sites, spoof sites	Overall: 67.7% Spoof detection: 93.5%
Trust Watch	None	Server-side blacklist	Spoof sites	Overall: 85.1% Spoof detection: 46.5%

Abbasi and Chen, 2009b.

PwdHash6replaces a user's password with a6one way hash of the password6and the domain6name (Ross et al., 2005). While6this is a simple technique to protect6against password phishing; it is not secure against6offline dictionary attacks, key6logger attacks, DNS6cache poisoning attacks, and cannot be6securely applied when the6user does not have6the privileges to install the tool on the6computer. Other anti-phishing6tools include6Google Safe Browsing (Schneider et al., 2009), SpoofStick (Dhamija et al., 2006), NetCraft tool bar (Ross et al., 2005), and SiteAdvisor (Provos et al., 2006). These are summarized in Table 2.2. Most of

Table 2.2 Anti-Phishing Tools

Tools	Prime feature	Limitations
Google Safe Browsing	Uses a blacklist of phishing URLs to identify a phishing site	Might not recognize phishing sites not present in the blacklist
NetCraft Tool Bar	Risk rating system used. Dominant factor in computing risk is age of the domain name.	Part of their technique involves using a database of sites, and hence might not recognize new phishing sites successfully.
SpoofStick	Provides basic domain information; on Ebay it will display *You are on ebay.com*, on a spoofed site it will display *You are on 20.240.10*	Not very effective against spoofed sites opened in multiple frames
SiteAdvisor	Primarily protects against spyware and adware attacks. Based on using bots to create a huge database of malware and test results on them to provide ratings for a site	As in the case of NetCraft, if a new phishing site does not have a rating in their database it might not be caught by this tool.

Garera et al., 2007.

these toolbars rely only on blacklist information and might not correctly identify new phishing attacks.

2.5.4 Ensemble System

Fusion methods of more than one classifier can be separated into three types depending on classifiers' output (Ruta and Gabrys, 2000). The first type is hard output or class-label output. The second type is class ranking output and the last type is soft output or fuzzy output.

Many researchers identified two main requirements for a successful ensemble (Toolan and Carthy, 2009). The first is accuracy, that the individual component classifiers of the ensemble must have a certain level of accuracy. The second is diversity, that the component classifiers must make sufficiently different errors. This is due to the fact that if all constituent classifiers make errors on the same instances then the ensemble will be unable to perform better than the best of the individual techniques (Toolan and Carthy, 2009).

Furthermore, Toolan and Carthy, 2009 introduced an approach to classifying emails into phishing/non-phishing categories using the C5.0 algorithm which achieves very high precision. The proposed classifier used a novel machine learning ensemble technique that is composed of a parent classifier (C5.0 in this case) with an ensemble of three learners (SVM, k-NN with k = 3 and k = 5) that achieve high recall are applied on the legitimate branch of the parent classifier. The primary motive behind this ensemble is to relabel false negatives to boost the true positives (or recall) rate. The proposed work achieved an f1-score of 99.31%. Also, the simple majority voting algorithm was chosen as such an odd number of constituent classifiers were required.

Airoldi and Malin (2004) employed three different learning methods to detect phishing scams. First, the emails were classified into three categories: spam, scam and ham (Figure 2.8). Figure 2.9 shows the relationship between the three categories.

The three algorithms (Naïve Bayes, Poisson, and K Nearest Neighbor) are then used for text classification. First, emails are classified into two categories of frauds and non-frauds using these algorithms. Then

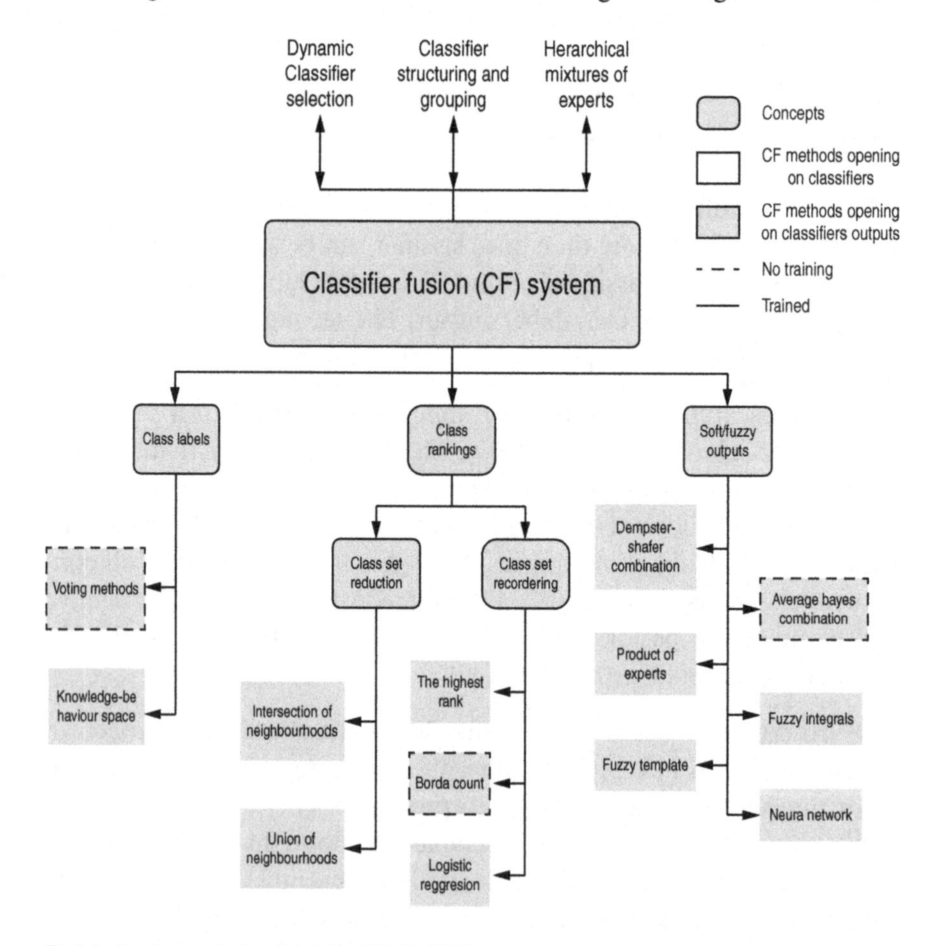

Fig. 2.8. Email categorization. (Airoldi and Malin, 2004)

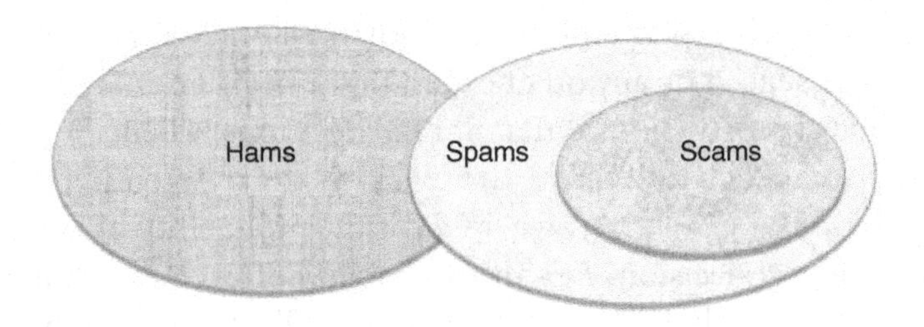

Fig. 2.9. Taxonomy of classifier fusion methods. (Zhang et al., 2006)

based on consensus method (Miyamoto et al., 2007), combining the results of the proposed data-mining algorithms, we improve the classification results. The aim of Saberi et al. (2007) is to use ensemble methods on their results to improve our scam detection mechanism. Then by using majority voting ensemble classification algorithm, their results were merged in order to increase the accuracy. Experimental results show that the proposed method in Saberi et al. (2007) can detect 94.4% of scam emails correctly, whereas only 0.08% of legitimate emails are classified as scams.

Toolan and Carthy (2009) refer to a fusion method with no training that was employed to reduce processing time. One of the ensemble algorithms chosen was the simple majority voting algorithm; as such an odd number of constituent classifiers were required. All sets of classifiers of size three were chosen for ensembles. The same algorithm will be used for voting in this book. Simple majority voting is further discussed below.

2.5.4.1 Simple Majority Vote

Rahman et al., 2002 proposed that if there are n independent experts having the same probability of being correct, and each of these experts produces a unique decision regarding the identity of the unknown sample, then the sample is assigned to the class for which there is a consensus, that is, when at least k of the experts agree, where k can be defined as:

$$K = \begin{cases} \frac{n}{2} + 1 \text{ if } n \text{ is even} \\ \frac{n+1}{2} \text{ if } n \text{ is odd} \end{cases} \tag{2.1}$$

Assuming each expert makes a decision on an individual basis, without being influenced by any other expert in the decision-making process, the probabilities of various different final decisions, when $x + y$ experts are trying to a reach a decision, are given by the different terms of the expansion of $(Pc + Pe)\ x + y$, where, Pc is the probability of each expert making a correct decision, $Pe$is the probability of each expert making a wrong decision, with $Pc + Pe = 1$. Bernoulli (Todhunter, 1865) is credited with first realizing this group decision distribution. The probability that x experts would arrive at the correct decision is $\frac{(x+y)!}{x!y!}(Pc)^x(Pe)^y$ and the probability that they arrive at the wrong decision is $\frac{(x+y)!}{x!y!}$ $(Pc)^y(Pe)^x$. So in general, the precondition of correctness (Berend and Paroush, 1998) of the combined decision for $x > y$ can be conveniently expressed as:

$$\mathrm{K} = \frac{(P_c)x(P_e)y}{(P_c)x(P_e)y + (P_c)y(P_e)x} \tag{2.2}$$

Reordering equation 2.2 and assuming the fraction of the experts arriving at the correct decision to be fixed, (e.g., x and y to be constant), it is possible to show that:

$$\frac{\delta k}{\delta P_c} = k^2 (x-y) \frac{(P_e)^{x-y-1}}{(P_c)^{x-y-1}} (P_c + P_e) \tag{2.3}$$

Since $(x - y - 1 \geq 0)$, $\frac{\delta k}{\delta P_c}$ is always positive. Thus when x and y are given, as Pc increases κ increases continuously from zero to unity. This demonstrates that the success of the majority voting scheme (like most decision combination schemes) directly depends on the reliability of the decision confidences delivered by the participating experts. It is also clear that as the confidences of the delivered decisions increase, the quality of the combined decision increases.

Recently, it has been demonstrated that although majority vote is by far the simplest of the variety of strategies used to combine multiple experts, if properly applied it can also be very effective. Suen et al. (1992) presented a method for decision combination incorporating different types of classifiers based on a straightforward voting scheme. A detailed study of the working of the majority voting scheme has been presented by Lam and Suen (1997) and Ng and Singh (1998) have discussed the applicability of majority voting techniques and have proposed a support function to be used in the combination of votes. Researchers have also used various types of classifiers in these majority voting schemes. Stajniak et al. (1997) presented a system having three voting nonlinear classifiers: two of them based on the multilayer perceptron (MLP), and one using the moments method. Parker (1995) has reported voting methods for multiple autonomous agents. Ji and Ma (1997) have reported a learning method to combine weak classifiers, where weak classifiers are linear classifiers (perceptron) which can do little better than making random guesses. The authors have demonstrated, both theoretically and experimentally, that if the weak classifiers are properly chosen, their combinations can achieve a good generalization performance with polynomial space-and time-complexity.

2.6 NORMALIZATION

As proposed by Al Shalabi and Shaaban (2006), data usually collected from multiple resources and stored in data warehouse may include multiple databases, data cubes, or flat files and as such could result to different issues arising during integration of data needed for mining and discovery. Such issues include scheme integration and redundancy. Therefore, data integration must be done carefully to avoid redundancy and inconsistency that in turn improves the accuracy and speed up the mining process (Jiawei and Kamber, 2001).

The careful data integration is now acceptable but it needs to be transformed into forms suitable for mining. Data transformation involves smoothing, generalization of the data, attribute construction, and normalization. The main purpose of data mining is to discover unrecognized associations between data items in an existing database. It is the process of extracting valid, previously unseen or unknown, comprehensible information from large databases. The growth of the size of data and number of existing databases exceeds the ability of humans to analyze this data, which creates both a need and an opportunity to extract knowledge from databases (Cios et al., 1998). Data transformation such as normalization may improve the accuracy and efficiency of mining algorithms involving neural networks, nearest neighbor, and clustering classifiers. Such methods provide better results if the data to be analyzed have been normalized, that is, scaled to specific ranges such as [0.0, 1.0] (Jiawei and Kamber, 2001).

Since both the data collection and feature extraction is done manually for this project, there is a margin for bogus range of numbers which might lead to inaccuracy in the output result and as such normalization of data is needed. Furthermore, to normalize the data into small number margin between "0s" and "1s," the use of rapidminer software (Akthar and Hahne, 2012) was adopted to create a model for normalization. First the dataset is converted into ".csv" and then imported into the software, where both the dataset and the normalization algorithm are linked and the output data collected and exported as ".csv."

An attribute is normalized by scaling its values so that they fall within a small-specified range, such as 0.0 to 1.0. Normalization is particularly useful for classification algorithms involving neural networks, or distance measurements such as nearest neighbor classification and clustering. If using the neural network back propagation algorithm for classification mining, normalizing the input values for each attribute measured in the training samples will help speed up the learning phase. For distanced-based methods, normalization helps prevent attributes with initially large ranges from outweighing attributes with initially smaller ranges (Jiawei and Kamber, 2001).

2.7 RELATED WORK

Although there are numerous studies in classifier fusion method in phishing website detection, but research on choosing the most effective ensemble system components for anti-phishing continues to be fresh. Table 2.3 presents some studies on existing anti-phishing system either for phishing website detection or in similar domains. In the figure that follows this study has consulted some studies that are quite related to the main study. These studies were found useful and have provided a focus for this study. These are based on the following headings: (1)title

Table 2.3 Related Studies

Title of the study	Author	Briefly description of study	Experimental results	Study limitations
Intelligent flushing website detection system using fuzzy techniques	(Aburrouse et al., 2008)	Tie proposed model is based on FL operators which is used to characterize me website flushing factors and indicators as fuzzy variables and produces six measures and criteria's of website phishing attack dimensions with a layer structure.	The experimental results showed me significance and importance of the phishing website criteria (URL Domain Identity) represented by layer one and the variety influence of the phishing characteristic layers on the final phishing website rate.	The approach does not look for deviations from stored patterns of normal phishing behavior and for previously described patterns of behavior that is likely to indicate phishing.
An anti-Phishing ppproach that uses training intervention for flushing websites detection is likely to indicate phishing.	(Ainajim and Munro, 2009)	This paper proposes and evaluates a novel anti-phishing approach that uses training intervention for Phishing websites detection (APTIPWD) in comparison to an existing approach (sending anti-phishing tips by emails) and control group.	There is a significant positive effect of using the APTIFWD in comparison on with the existing approach and control group in helping users properly judging legitimate and phishing websites.	Nil
Identifying vulnerable websites by analysis of common strums in phishing URLs	(Wardmaner et al., 2009)	The propos ed method involves applying a –longest common substring algorithm to known phishing URLs, and investigating me results of that string to identify common vulnerabilities, exploits, and attack tools which may be prevalent among those who lack servers for phishing.	The result demonstrated mat these application paths may be used as a basis for further investigation to expose and document the primary exploits and tools used by hackers to compromise web servers, which could lead to the revelation of the aliases or identities of me criminals.	Nil
Associative classification techniques for predicting e-banking phishing websites	(Aburrous et al., 2010)	The research proposed an intelligent, resilient aid effective model that is based on using association and classification data mining algorithms. They used a number of different listing data mining association and classification techniques	The experimental results demonstrated me feasibility of using associative classification techniques in real applications and its better performance as compared to other traditional classifications algorithms.	Nil

of the study (2) names of author (3) brief descriptions of the studies (4) the experimental results, and (5) study limitations.

Some studies have applied K-Nearest Neighbour (KNN) for phishing website classification. KNN classifier is a non-parametric classification algorithm. The major disadvantage of this classifier is that the accuracy falls with increase in the size of the training set. In addition, previous researches have shown that KNN can achieve very accurate results, that are sometimes more accurate than those of the symbolic classifiers. It was shown in a study carried out by Kim and Huh, 2011 that KNN classifier achieved the best result compared to other classifier such as linear discriminate analysis (LDA), naıve Bayesian (NB), and support vector machine (SVM). In the study, they collected 10000 items of routing information in total: 5000 from 50 highly targeted websites (100 per website) representing the legitimate samples; and the other 5000 from 500 phishing websites (10 per website) representing the DNS-poisoning-based phishing samples. The initial dataset for phishing websites was obtained from a community website called PhishTank. An accuracy detection rate of about 99% was achieved. Also, since the performance of KNN is primarily determined by the choice of K, they tried to find the best K by varying it from 1 to 5; and found that KNN performs best when K = 1. This as well, helped in the high accuracy of KNN compared to other classifiers ensemble.

Artificial neural network (ANN) consists of a collection of processing elements that are highly interconnected and transform a set of inputs to a set of desired outputs. The result of the transformation is determined by the characteristics of the elements and the weights associated with the interconnections among them. Since neural network gains experience over a period as it is being trained on the data related to the problem, the major disadvantage is in the time it takes for parameter selection and network learning. On the other hand, previous researches have shown that ANN can achieve very accurate results compared to other learning classification techniques. In a research carried out by Basnet et al. (2008), it was shown that artificial neural network achieved an accuracy of 97.99% using a dataset of 4000 phishing samples that was divided equally between training sample and testing sample; each having a sample of 2000.

2.8 SUMMARY

This chapter covered important aspects of phishing. These are: the primary idea of phishing, existing anti-phishing techniques and approaches, and different designs of classifiers. This chapter has also covered website phishing detection plus some previous works at length. It further describes the particular issues faced by anti-phishing tools and pointed out some existing solutions for every one too. These problems pose challenges in the study regarding efficiency of anti-phishing tools. It had been proven that the majority of the literature was unsuccessful in eliminating the false positive rates, even when there is a relatively high detection rate. The issue of phishing detection using blacklist seemed to be outlined in certain studies due to increasing evolution of phishers. Other studies demonstrated the importance of combining the right set of classifiers in ensemble system is extremely important in achieving good detection results. Additionally, this research is concerned with detection rate of phishing website using different classifiers in ensemble and comparison with individual classifiers.

CHAPTER 3

Research Methodology

3.1 INTRODUCTION

It is a classification of systematic work achieved via series of steps, which is used as guideline throughout a research, in order to accomplish the objectives of the research. This study focuses on a comparison between an ensemble system and classifier system in website phishing detection which are ensemble of classifiers (C5.0, SVM, LR, KNN) and individual classifiers. The aim is to investigate the effectiveness of each algorithm to determine accuracy of detection and false alarms rate. So, this chapter will provide a clear guideline on how the research's goals and objectives shall be achieved. This chapter also discusses the dataset used in this study.

3.2 RESEARCH FRAMEWORK

Research framework will be for implementing the steps taken throughout the research. It is normally used as a guide for researchers so that they are more focused in the scope of their studies. Figure 3.1 shows an operational framework that will be followed in this study.

Overview of Research Framework

The study is divided into three phases and each phase's output is an input to the next phase. Phase-1 is based on dataset processing and feature extraction. Phase-2 is based on evaluating individual reference classifiers that involve training and testing using precision, recall, accuracy, and F1-score. Phase-3a is aimed to evaluate the ensemble of all the classifiers using precision, recall, accuracy, and F1-score. Phase-3b compares the result from the two techniques (individual and ensemble) in highlighting the better technique for phishing website detection based on the output of precision, recall, accuracy, and F1-score. These phases are depicted in the Figure 3.1.

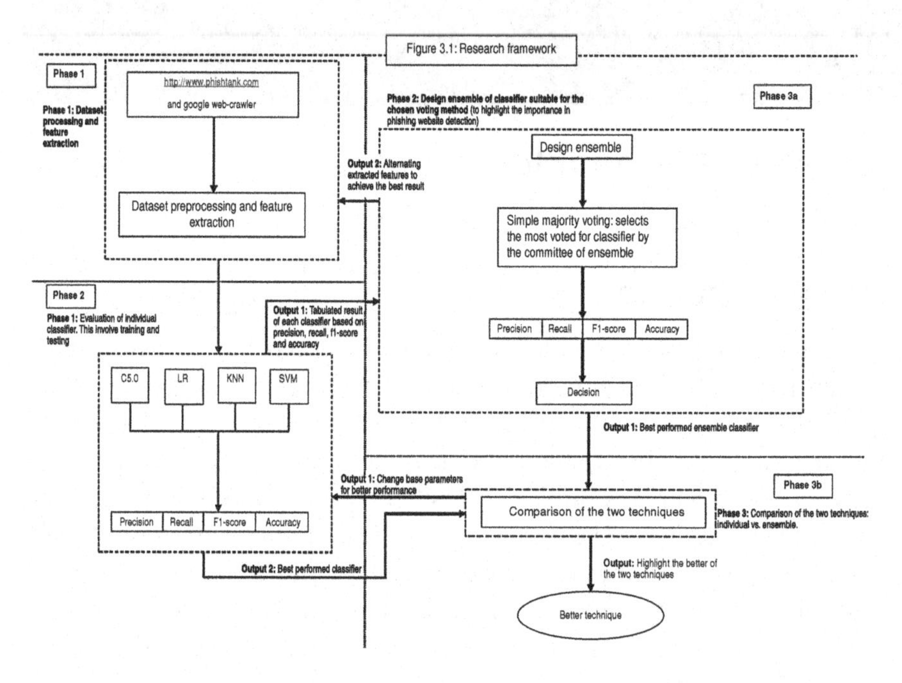

Fig. 3.1. Research framework.

3.3 RESEARCH DESIGN

The research will be conducted through three main phases. The following subsections will describe each phase briefly.

3.3.1 Phase 1: Dataset Processing and Feature Extraction

The processing of dataset was carried out on the collected datasets to better refine them to the requirement of the study. Many stages are involved in processing, some of this are: feature extraction, normalization, dataset division, and attribute weighting. These are very necessary in ensuring that the classifier can understand the dataset and properly classify them into the reference classes. The output of this phase is directly passed on to Phase 2 in evaluation the reference classifiers.

3.3.2 Phase 2: Evaluation of Individual Classifier

Evaluation of classifiers is required in this research to measure the performance achieved by a learning algorithm. To do this, a test set consisting of dataset with known labels is used. Each of the classifier is trained with a training set, applied to the test set, and then measured the performance of

Table 3.1 Formula Used to Calculate the Performance

Performance Measure		Description
Percentage % classification	Accuracy	Accuracy is the overall correctness of the model and is calculated as the sum of correct classifications divided by the total number of classifications $\frac{TN+TP}{TN+TP+FN+FP}$
	Precision	Precision is a measure of the accuracy provided that a specific class has been predicted $\frac{TP}{TP+FP}$
	Recall/true positive rate (TPR)/ detection rate (DR)	Measuring the frequency of the correctly detected patterns as normal by the classifier. $\frac{TP}{TP+FN}$
	F1 Score	F1 score (also F-score or F-measure) is a measure of a test's accuracy. The F1 score can be interpreted as a weighted average of the precision and recall, where an F1 score reaches its best value at 1 and worst score at 0. The traditional F-measure or balanced F-score is the harmonic mean of precision and recall: $2 \cdot \frac{precision \cdot recall}{precision+recall}$
Error percentage (%)	False positive rate (FPR) known as false alarm rate (FAR)	The average of normal patterns wrongly classified as malicious patterns. $\frac{FP}{TN+FP}$
	False negative rate (FNR)	The average of malicious patterns mistakenly classified as normal patterns. $\frac{FN}{FP+FN}$
Elkan, 2008.		

by comparing the predicted labels with the true labels (that were not available to the training algorithm) (Elkan, 2008). Therefore, it is important to evaluate the classifiers by training and testing with the dataset obtained from Phase 1 using the following performance metrics; precision, recall, f1-score, and accuracy. The formula used is shown in Table 3.1.

Table 3.2 Classification Context

	Actual class (observation)	
Expected class (expectation)	TP	FP
	(True positive)	(False positive)
	Correct result	Unexpected result
	FN	TN
	(False negative)	(True negative)
	Missing result	Correct absence of result

3.3.2.1 Classification Background

In order to properly understand the classification notations used in Table 3.1, a brief explanation of the notations will be discussed in this section with the aid of Table 3.2 that shows the relationship between the actual class and the expected class.

Based on notations in Table 3.2;

1. Let TP represent the number of legitimate website correctly classified as legitimate.
2. Let TN represent the number of websites classified correctly as phishing website.
3. Let FP represent the number of legitimate websites classified as phishing website.
4. Let FN represent the number of websites classified as legitimate websites when they were actually phishing websites.

3.3.2.2 Classifier Performance

In this section, the process of detecting the performance of each classifier will be discussed. All classifiers will be evaluated based on the metrics (precision, recall, f1 score, and accuracy) already illustrated in Table 3.1. Furthermore, each of these classifiers will be introduced in this section in terms of performance.

3.3.2.2.1 C5.0 Algorithm

C5.0 is a decision tree algorithm used to measure the disorder in the collection of attribute and effectiveness of an attribute using entropy and information gain, respectively. The operation of C5.0 on the dataset can be categorized into two equations:

1. Calculating the entropy value of the data using the equation below:

$$E(S)=\sum_{i=1}^{c}-p_1 log_2 p_1 \quad (3.1)$$

Where E(S) – entropy of a collection of dataset, c – represents the number of classes in the system and p_i – represents the number of instances proportion that belongs to class i.

2. Calculating the information gain for an attribute C, in a collection S, where E(S) is the entropy of the whole collection and S_w is the set of instances that have value w for attribute C.

$$G(S,C)=E(S)-\sum_{w\in \, values\,(C)}\frac{S_w}{S}E(S_w) \quad (3.2)$$

Figure 3.2 shows the structure of a decision tree that partitions the dataset on the given attribute in order to calculate the information gain.

3.3.2.2.2 K-Nearest Neighbour

KNN employs the use of Euclidean Distance. It is based on the premise that every instance in the dataset can be represented as a point in *N*-dimensional space. Also, KNN uses a value *K* to represent the number of instances to be used after which the majority class will be chosen to classify

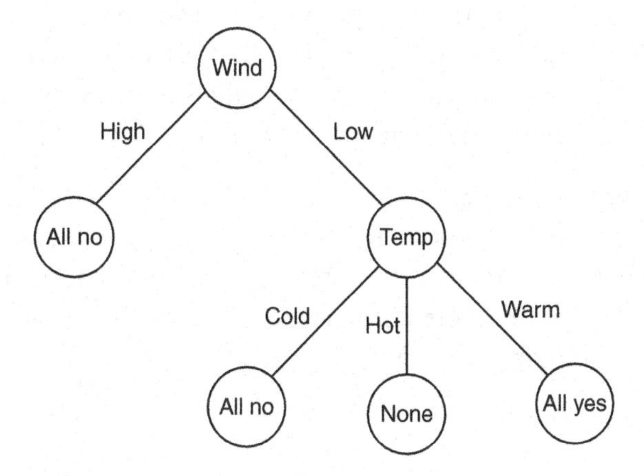

Fig. 3.2. Decision tree structure.

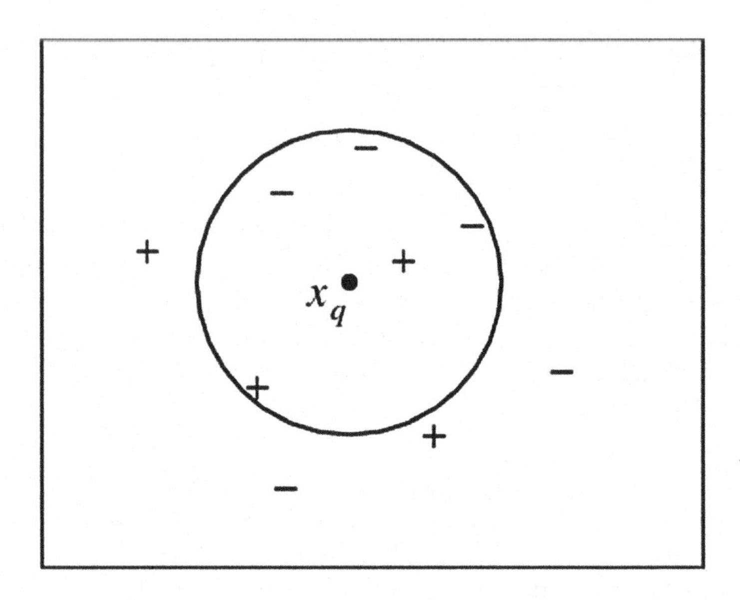

Fig. 3.3. KNN structure.

the new instance. Figure 3.3, shows the structure of K-Nearest Neighbour algorithm. Equation (3.3) shows the formula used in the algorithm:

$$d(x_i, x_j) = \sqrt{\sum_{r-1}^{n} \left(a_r(x_i) - a_r(x_j)\right)^2} \tag{3.3}$$

3.3.2.2.3 Support Vector Machine (SVM)

SVN is basically suitable for binary classification. It is based on a principle similar to KNN in that it represents the training set as points in an *N*-dimensional space and then attempts to construct a hyperplane that will divide the space into particular class labels with a precise margin of error. Figure 3.4 shows the structure of Support Vector Machine.

3.3.2.2.4 Linear Regression

Linear regression attempts to use a formula to generate a real-valued attribute. This method uses discrete value for prediction by setting a threshold *T* on the predicted real value. Equation (3.4) shows the formula used by linear regression

$$c = w_0 + \sum_{i=1}^{A} w_i \times a_i \tag{3.4}$$

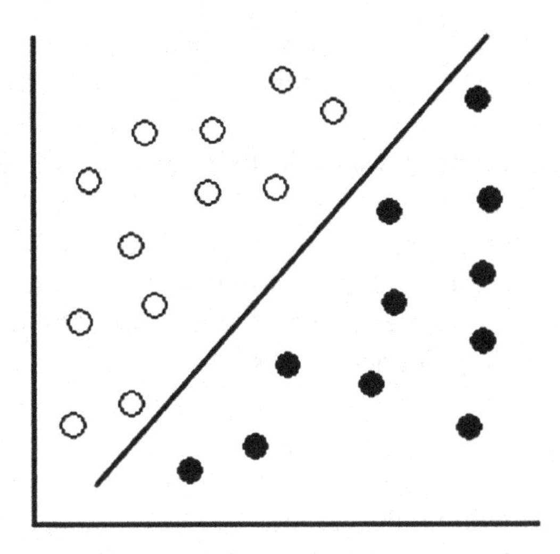

Fig. 3.4. SVM structure.

3.3.3 Phase 3a: Evaluation of Classifier Ensemble

Classifier ensemble was proposed to improve the classification performance of a single classifier (Kittler et al., 1998). The classifiers trained and tested in Phase 1 are used in this phase to determine the ensemble design. Also, this phase is divided into two subphases, that is, Phase 3a and Phase 3b.

Simple majority voting is used to ensemble the classifiers in determining detection accuracy. This is an iterative phase in which a threshold (acceptable detection accuracy set) is set and checked with the evaluation results until an optimum result is achieved. Equation (3.5) shows the formula for calculating detection accuracy.

$$Detection\,Accuracy\,Result = (a \times d_1) + (b \times d_2) + (c \times d_3) \qquad (3.5)$$

Where a + b + c = 1 and a, b, and c are variables in the range of [0,1]

Phase 3a is divided into two parts, namely design and decision. In the design part, four algorithms are being considered for ensemble and a committee of three algorithms is used to form an ensemble since majority voting requires an odd number of participants. On the basis of the output of Phase 2, all the individual algorithms will be evaluated with the same metrics used in Phase 2 and then voted on. The decision part of Phase 3a rely on the output of the design part to decide which of the ensemble is the best performed which is then passed to Phase 3b for comparison with the best of the four algorithms evaluated in Phase 2.

3.3.4 Phase 3b: Comparison of Individual versus Ensemble Technique

In this part, the comparison of the two techniques discussed in Phase 2 and Phase 3a is carried out. The results obtained from the previously discussed phases are used as input for this phase. The results are then compared using tables and rich graphs.

3.4 DATASET

The dataset used will be divided into two parts namely, phishing and non-phishing dataset. The phishing dataset will be collected from phishtank whereas the non-phish dataset have been collected manually using Google engine. Dataset from Phishtank is discussed below:

3.4.1 Phishtank

Phishtank is a phish website repository available to users for free (open source). Because of the public nature of Phishtank with lots of suspected phish websites being submitted frequently, their database is updated by the hour and as such a total of 7,612 phish websites were obtained that have been accumulated over a period of 4 years since January 2008. Though as it has studied by several researchers that most phishing websites are only for temporary use, some of this websites have been reported offline. A filtration process is thus needed to ensure the freshness of the dataset. After this filtration had been done, 3611 phishing websites were confirmed online. This fresh dataset is used as phishing website for

Table 3.3 Phishtank Statistics

Online, valid phishes	Total submissions	Total votes
13,054	1,615,087	6,362,861

Phishes verified as valid		Suspected phishes submitted	
Total	988,254	Total	1,615,088
Online	13,054	Online	13,463
Offline	975,200	Offline	1,599,398

the purpose of this study. Table 3.3 shows the statistics collected from Phishtank as at the time of data collection.

3.5 SUMMARY

This chapter comprises of the methodology used as described in previous sections. Section 3.3.1 described the dataset processing and feature extraction, Section 3.3.2 described how individual classifiers will be evaluated using different metrics (precision, accuracy, recall, and f1-score). Section 3.3.3 described how the ensemble design is used in choosing the best ensemble classifier through decision-making process. Section 3.3.4 described the comparison process of selecting the better of the two techniques for website phishing detection. Finally, Section 3.4 described the dataset used in this study.

CHAPTER 4

Feature Extraction

4.1 INTRODUCTION

This chapter covers the dataset mode of collection and preparation including the extraction of all of the features intended for use in this study. Phishtank repository is used as the only source of phishing dataset whereas the non-phish dataset is collected manually using Google search engine. Basically, the output from feature extraction will be used as input in evaluating the individual classifiers as discussed in the phases of Chapter 3. Further sections of this chapter will discuss the feature extraction process as follows: Section 4.2 discusses the data processing procedures including the dataset statistics. Furthermore, subsections of Section 4.2 discuss the feature extraction process, data verification, data normalization; method and criteria used for normalization. Section 4.3 discusses the dataset division; in terms of dataset grouping and the percentage of phishing and non-phishing dataset used with justification in order to increase the performance of the classifier training process to better improve the accuracy of the result. Finally, Section 4.4 discuss the summary of the chapter and the also discuss the accomplishment of this chapter in accordance to the objectives of this project.

4.2 DATASET PROCESSING

In order to realize a dataset suitable for the purpose of this project, the phish data collected from Phishtank was reorganized and some derived features were added. Also the dataset format that was downloaded from Phishtank repository had to be changed from dot csv format (.csv) to SQL database format (.sql) in order to make it acceptable for use with php. Because of the open source nature of Phishtank, most of the features needed for this project were not included and as such most features were extracted manually using php code. In the dataset collected from Phishtank, some of the features such as "phish_detail_url," "submission_time," "verified," "verification_time," and "online" were excluded

Table 4.1 Dataset Statistic

	Phishing websites	Non-phishing websites
Total collected	7612	1638
Offline	3999	0
Tested alive	3611	1638

and new features extracted and added to the dataset. After the extraction of features, normalization of dataset is then carried out using rapidminer (Akthar and Hahne, 2012) for easy computation. Table 4.1 shows the statistics of dataset used. Here, both the phishing and non-phishing websites have been tested for alive properties making sure that the data to be used must be correct and available for further step which is feature extraction. Meanwhile, Figure 4.1 shows the pie graph of the percentage of phishing to non-phishing data used in the study.

4.2.1 Feature Extraction

This section focuses on the effective minimal set of features that can be utilized in detecting phishing website (Figure 4.2). As summarized in Section 4.2, the features were manually extracted from the dataset using php code will be discussed in this section. First, the dataset for phishing website is downloaded from Phishtank (OpenDNS), tested to confirm it is online and then the features are extracted from each website. For non-phishing website, a webcrawler is used to extract the dataset

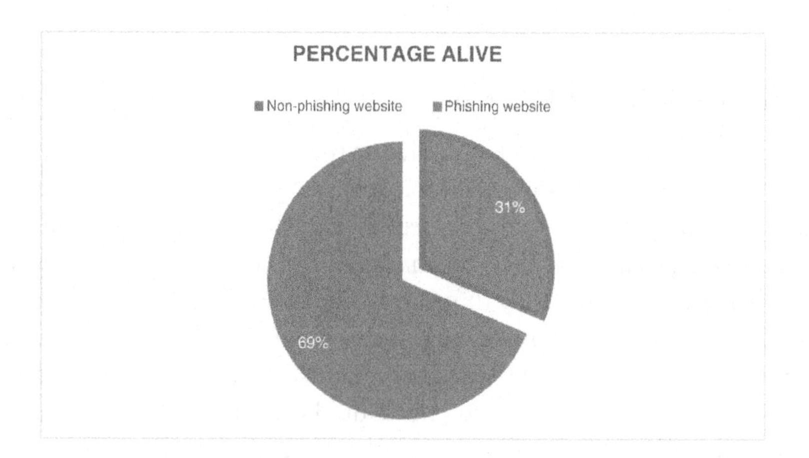

Fig. 4.1. Percentage phishing to non-phishing.

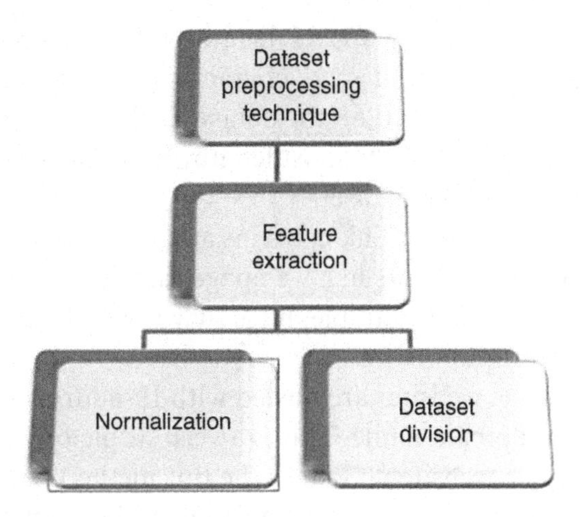

Fig. 4.2. Overview of feature extraction.

from Google and also manual extraction was done using Google search engine and then the source code is extracted using php code in phpmyadmin webserver (Anewalt and Ackermann, 2005). The features extracted for each of the two scenarios (phishing and non-phishing) was carefully extracted from previous research work based on their individual weight. A combination of the features used in the work of Garera et al. (2007) and Zhang et al. (2007) is used for carefully selecting the features to be extracted. These features have proven very efficient in the detection of phishing websites (Huang et al., 2012). Furthermore, the features are labeled from 1 to 10 and they are termed as f_1, f_2, f_3,.. and f_{10}. The 10th column labeled f10 is the classification label of the dataset as phishing or non-phishing shown in equation (4.1).

Each of this features are explained briefly to support the claim of their importance in website phishing detection in relation to previous researches.

4.2.2 Extracted Features

1. **Long URL**: Long URL's can be used to hide the suspicious part of in the address bar. Although scientifically there is reliable method of predicting the range of length that justify a website as phishing or non-phishing but then it is criteria used with other features in detecting suspicious sites. In the study of Basnet et al. (2011), a proposed length of ≤ 75 but there was no justification for behind

their value. In this project a URL length of >127 character is used for non-phishing and ≤127 character for phishing website. This value is chosen based on the dataset collected by manually comparing the length of the most lengthy non-phishing website and phishing website in the dataset.

2. **Dots:** A secure web-page link contains at most 5 dots. If perhaps, there are more than 5 dots in a web page then it may be recognized as a phishing link. For example: http://www.website1.com.my/www.phish.com/index.php
3. **IP-address:** Some websites are hosted with IP-address instead of a fully qualified domain name. This is a very suspicious act since most of the legitimate website no longer use this method because of security reasons. Also, since most phishing websites stay online for a limited time, this feature can be considered as one of the very relevant phishing detection features.
4. **SSL connection:** It is necessary for a payment or e-commerce payment site to be secured in such that the data transmitted from and to the website is encrypted. Also it can be used to confirm the identity of a website by using SSL certificate which include specific information regarding the website. A sample from one of the non-phishing website collected is shown in Figure 4.3.
5. **At "@" symbol:** the phishing URL may include the "@" symbol somewhere within the address because the web browser, when reading an internet address; ignore everything to the left of the @ symbol, therefore, the address ebay.com@fake-auction.com would actually be "fake-auction.com."

   Hexadecimal: Particular to phishing are hex-encoded URLs. In the interest of compatibility, most mail user agents, web browsers, and HTTP servers all understand basic hex-encoded character

Fig. 4.3. URL with secure socket layer.

equivalents, so that: http://210.219.241.125/images/paypal/cgi-bin/webscrcmd_login.php and http://%32%31%30.%32%31%39%2e%32%34%31%2e%31%32%35/%69%6d%61%67%65%73/paypal/cgi-bin/webscrcmd_login.php are functionally equivalent. The main illicit purpose of this encoding is to evade blacklist-based anti-spam filters which do not process hex character encoding (effectively, another insertion attack). It also evades protection mechanisms that prohibit IP addresses as URL destinations, on the assumption that "normal" http links will use more familiar DNS names.

6. **Frame**: Frames are a popular method of hiding attack content due to their uniform browser support and easy coding style. Example shown in Figure 4.3 describes a scenario in which the attacker defines two frames. The first frame contains the legitimate site URL information, whereas the second frame – occupying 0% of the browser interface that has a malicious code running. The page linked within the hidden frame can be used to deliver additional content, retrieving confidential information such as Session ID' s or something more advance such as executing screen-grabbing and key-logging while the user is exchanging confidential information over the Internet. The output of Figure 4.4 is shown in Figure 4.5.

Redirect: A web application accepts a user-controlled input that specifies a link to an external site, and uses that link in a redirect. This simplifies phishing attacks. For example, "www.facebook.com/l/53201;phish.com." This will redirect the page to phish.com, using "facebook" as a redirect site. Since "facebook" is a common social

```
<html>
<head>
<title>Frame Based Exploit Example</title>
</head>

<body topmargin="0" leftmargin="0" rightmargin="0" bottommargin="0">
<iframe src="http://www.yahoo.com" width="100%" height="150" frameborder="0">
</iframe>
<iframe src="http://www.msn.com" width="100%" height="350" frameborder="0">
</iframe>
</body>
</html>
```

Fig. 4.4. Source code for frame embedded website.

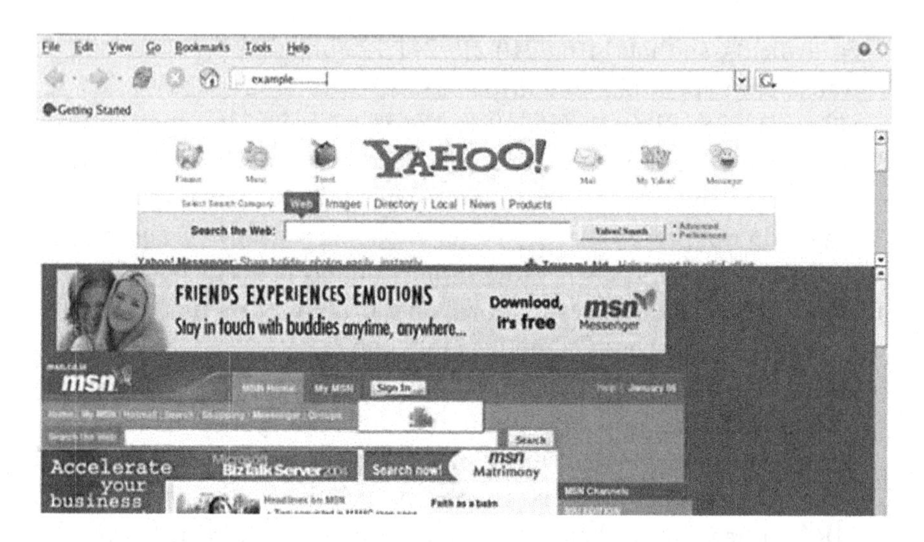

Fig. 4.5. Output of frame embedded website scenario.

network site, the assumption of a user before clicking on the link is that the website contains "facebook" at the beginning and definitely end up in "facebook" website but perhaps, if the website link were to begin with "www.phish-facebook.com" the user becomes suspicious.

Submit: Phishing websites often include "submit" button in their source code which most often than none, contains an address to the phisher's email or a database. When the user, thinking the website is a legitimate one, enter private information, and click the submit button, either a page cannot be found or some other error messages appear on the screen and mostly the user can assume it is a network problem of some sort. This is common in most duplicate website phishing scenario.

Figure 4.6 shows the flowchart of the feature extraction process indicating each feature as a variable and the conditions met for individual feature classification.

In Figure 4.6, each F_i represent a step. Assuming each step is labeled S_i where i is a correspondence of both F and S. The range of $i = \{1, 2 \ldots, 9\}$ and for every i, a feature F_i is extracted and checked to confirm if it satisfies the criterion in the decision box. If steps $S_{i=(1\ldots9)}$ fail to recognize a phishing threat, then the URL will be saved in the non-phish database for further data-mining.

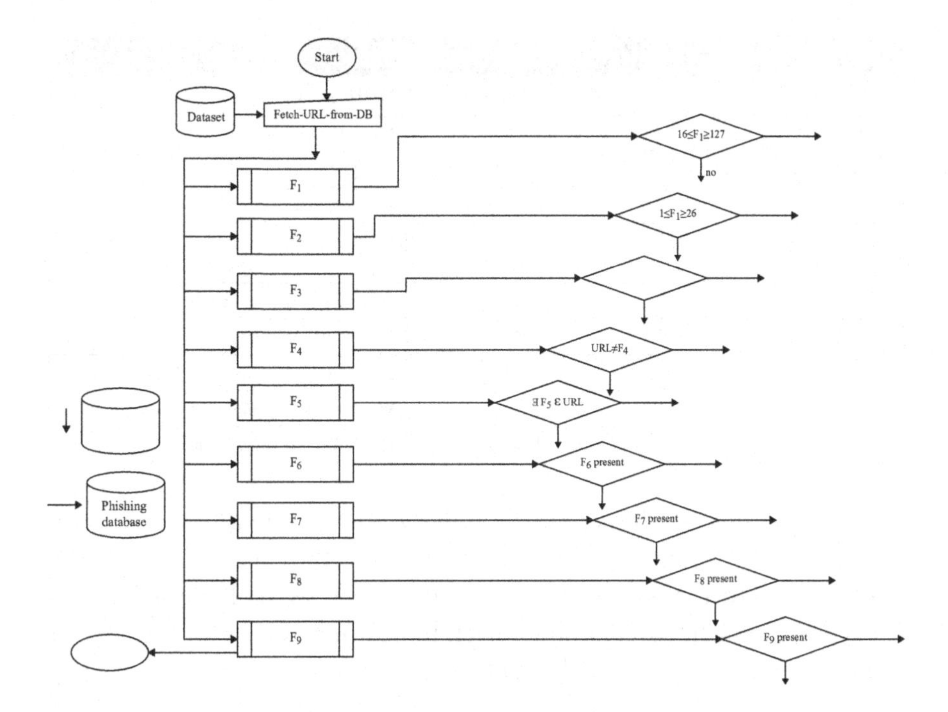

Fig. 4.6. Feature extraction process flow-chart.

The dataset is sorted and saved in a database which is later exported for further analysis. Table 4.2 shows the features and the terms used: the terms are used for simplicity in describing and referring to each of the features.

Table 4.2 Dataset Features

Features	Terms	Description
long_url	f1	Bogus URL address
Dots	f2	Excessive Dots in URL address
ip_address	f3	Using IP-address instead of a registered domain
ssl connection	f4	Secure (encryption) protocol for communication with the web server
at symbol	f5	Presence of '@' sign in the URL address
Hexadecimal	f6	The URL is masked with hexadecimal code
Frame	f7	Frame component of html code
Redirect	f8	Webpage with redirect link
Submit	f9	Webpage including submit button
Classification	f10	Value assigned to classes
Garera et al., 2007; Zhang et al., 2007.		

Table 4.3 Feature Categorization under Phishing Indicators

Criteria	N	Terms	Phishing indicator
URL and domain identity	1	f_3	Using IP address
Security and encryption		f_4	Using SSL certificate
Source code and Java Script	3	f_8	Redirect pages
Page style *and* content	1	f_7	Empty page reference of other browser pages
	2	f_9	Using forms with submit button
Web address bar	1	f_1	Long URL addresses
	2	f_2	Excessive dots in a URL address
	3	f_5	Website links containing "@" symbol
	4	f_6	IP address masking with hexadecimal code

Based on case studies conducted, the 9 extracted features were categorized under 5 indicators. This indicators show the class of each feature with respect to the composition of a typical website. Table 4.3 shows the features as categorized under each indicator where *N* represents the number of features classified under each criterion.

4.2.3 Data Verification

Data collected manually needs to be verified in order to ascertain the alive status especially in the case of phishing as it is known that phishing website mostly last for a limited period of time. For this reason, each URL must be verified before processing.

4.2.4 Data Normalization

There are many methods for data normalization that include min–max normalization (range transformation), z-score normalization, and normalization by decimal scaling. Min–max normalization performs a linear transformation on the original data. Suppose that min_a and max_a are the minimum and the maximum values for attribute A. Min–max normalization maps a value *v* of *A* to *v'* in the range ($new\text{-}min_a$, $new\text{-}max_a$) by computing as shown in equation (4.1). To customize the normalization output to desired scale, range transformation method was selected. Equation (4.1) shows the range transformation formula used for normalization:

$$v' = \left(\frac{(v - min_a)}{(max_a - min_a)}\right) * \left((new - max_a) - (new - min_a)\right) + new - min_a \tag{4.1}$$

ip_address	ssl_connection	long_url	dots	at_symbo	hexadecimal	frame	redirect	submit
0	0	72	3	0	0	0	0	1
0	0	232	5	0	0	0	0	1
0	0	56	3	0	0	0	0	1
0	0	173	5	0	0	0	0	1
0	0	35	2	0	0	0	0	1
0	0	220	2	0	0	0	0	1
0	0	45	2	0	0	0	0	1
0	0	135	3	0	0	0	0	1
0	0	218	4	0	0	0	0	1

Fig. 4.7. Dataset before normalization.

The extracted features are set to values described in the rule set shown in equation (4.3) below where $i = n$ and $n \in 1, n+1, \ldots, 9$.

In order to show the need for normalization of the dataset, Figures 4.7 and 4.8 show the dataset before and after normalization, respectively.

In Figure 4.7, the columns outlined (in red in the online version of the book) contains large numbers as compared to the other cells and as such normalization of this data is needed in order to prevent inaccuracy of results. The normalized data is shown in Figure 4.8.

4.3 DATASET DIVISION

After data processing, the dataset is divided into three sets for training and testing purpose and to investigate the accuracy of result. Two steps of data division are used, the first step is to divide the data into three different groups, and then choose different percentage of phishing and non-phishing for each group, for first group 50% phishing and

ip_address	ssl_connection	long_url	dots	at_symbol	hexadecimal	frame	redirect	submit
0	0	0.229437	0.076923	0	0	0	0	1
0	0	0.922078	0.153846	0	0	0	0	1
0	0	0.160173	0.076923	0	0	0	0	1
0	0	0.666667	0.153846	0	0	0	0	1
0	0	0.069264	0.038462	0	0	0	0	1
0	0	0.87013	0.038462	0	0	0	0	1
0	0	0.112554	0.038462	0	0	0	0	1
0	0	0.502165	0.076923	0	0	0	0	1
0	0	0.861472	0.115385	0	0	0	0	1

Fig. 4.8. Dataset after normalization.

Table 4.4 Total Data for Each Group and Each Process

Datasets	No. of phishing	No. of non-phishing
Set-A: 1750 instances (phishing)	525 (30%)	1225 (70%)
Set-B: 1750 instances (phishing)	875 (50%)	875 (50%)
Set-C: 1750 instances (phishing)	1225 (70%)	525 (30%)

remaining 50% non-phishing, second group 70% phishing and 30% non-phishing, and the last group 30% phishing and 70% are non-phishing as shown in Table 4.4. Furthermore, a cross-validation of 10% is used to estimate predictive performance of the selected attribute set is used (Hall et al., 2009).

Table 4.4 shows the total dataset and the division across phishing and non-phishing dataset. Also, it shows the number of instances covered for each process.

Finally, the prepared input and target output is tested and trained using stratified sample type method and a cross-validation of 10-folds which was selected after (10, 20, …, 90) folds have been tested and the standard deviation calculated. The data set is divided into k subsets, and the holdout method is repeated k times. Each time, one of the k subsets is used as the test set and the other k-1 subsets are put together to form a training set. Dataset for training process is used to train the NN model in identifying the pattern of data. Dataset for testing process is used to test the ability of network in identifying the pattern.

4.4 SUMMARY

Chapter 4 has described the process of data collection, feature extraction, data normalizing, and description of the extracted features. The output of this chapter is a direct input for the Phase 1 in research methodology. The purpose is to preprocess the data for usability in achieving the objectives of this project.

CHAPTER 5

Implementation and Result

5.1 INTRODUCTION

The process of dataset processing, feature selection, and dataset division was presented in Chapter 4. This chapter addresses the problem of selecting the best classification technique for website phishing detection that causes degradation in detection accuracy and high false alarm rate. The main objective of this chapter is to train and test the individual reference classifiers (C5.0, LR, KNN, and SVM) with the same dataset, design an ensemble of the reference classifiers, and compare the ensemble classifier performance with the best single classifier performance to choose the better of the two performances to overcome the low classification rate in website phishing detection. One of the major contributing factors to low overall accuracy is the selection of weak weighted features for classification. The situation worsens when a lazy algorithm is trained and tested with a large dataset. Therefore, the performance of the research methodology used in this project may not perform so well if the wrong classifier is trained and tested with dataset size more than the classifier's capacity.

The solution and research activities discussed in this chapter are identified in Phase 2 and Phase 3 in the overall research plan in Chapter 3. The chapter begins with an overview of the investigation and then followed by details of investigations on training and testing model for the reference classifiers. Furthermore, the operational procedure and algorithm for the investigated models are provided. Performance metrics are presented in terms of detection accuracy, precision, recall, and F-score. Finally, overall discussion on the result and a summary concludes the chapter.

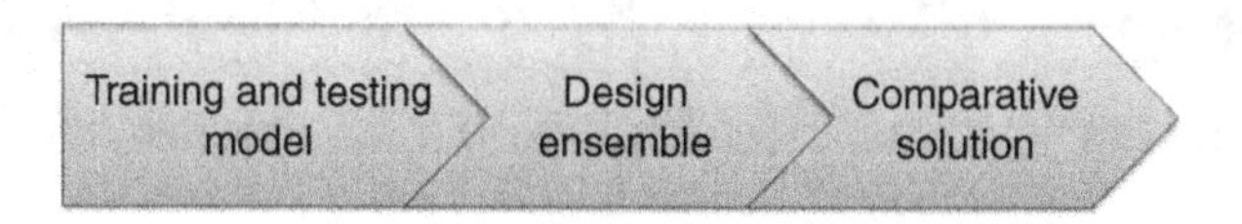

Fig. 5.1. An overview of the investigation towards selecting the best classification technique for website phishing detection.

5.2 AN OVERVIEW OF THE INVESTIGATION

The investigation in this chapter can be divided into three main parts, namely training and testing, design ensemble, and finally comparative solution. Figure 5.1 shows an overview of the investigations conducted in this chapter.

Training and testing model refers to the procedure involved in learning the algorithms with part of the dataset and testing the performance of the algorithms in correctly classifying the dataset. Meanwhile, design ensemble refers to the process of taking the output classifier performance of individual classifier in ensemble. Although, there are different ways of classifier ensemble, majority voting was used for this process. This is based on the assumption that the error rate of each classifier is less than 0.5 and errors made by classifiers are uncorrelated. Hence, the probability that the ensemble classifier makes a wrong prediction is considerably low. Finally, the results obtained for both individual classifier and ensemble design were compared.

5.2.1 Experimental Setup

Experiments were performed with 4061 (1638 non-phishing = 31% and 3611 phishing = 69%) instances of which all were manually classified as phishing or non-phishing. After selecting all the attributes (nine regular attributes, one binominal class label) the last column of data represents whether the URL is considered phishing (1) or not (0). The attributes indicates if there are any irregular patterns in the classification results obtained during implementation of the algorithms. All the nine attributes' statistical measure and definition are as follows:

1. Continuous real [0, 1] attributes of type attributes
2. Two continuous real [0, −1] attributes of type attributes
3. One binominal (0, 1) class attribute of type phish = denotes whether the URL was considered phishing (1) or not (0).

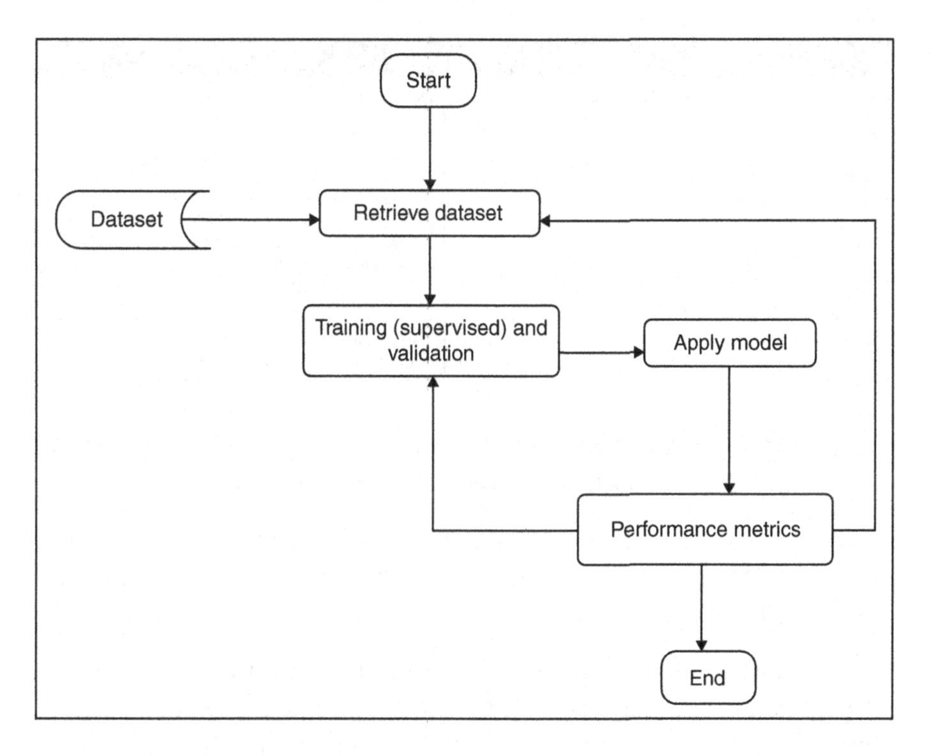

Fig. 5.2. Procedure for training and testing model (baseline).

4. Three datasets are used. This datasets are named Set A, Set B, and Set C as discussed in dataset division section in Chapter 4.

5.3 TRAINING AND TESTING MODEL (BASELINE MODEL)

Training and testing model is also termed as baseline model in this book. This model serves as a baseline for selecting the best ensemble classifier discussed in Section 5.4. Furthermore the baseline model output serve as one of the input for the process discussed in Section 5.5. Figure 5.2 shows the procedure of training and testing model.

In this design, the "retrieve dataset" process will retrieve the one of the three datasets at a time and pass it over to the "training and validation" process where x-validation used and the model applied for training. The most important component of this model are the reference classifiers used for each loop from the "performance metric" to "training and validation." Also, the "performance metric" loop back to "retrieve

Table 5.1 Key Parameters Values Used in Training and Testing Process

Parameter	Value/Quantity	Description
K	1	Finding the *k* training examples that are closest to the unseen example is the first step of the k-NN algorithm
Sampling type	Stratified sampling	Builds random subsets and ensures that the class distribution in the subsets is the same as in the whole reference dataset
No. of validations	10	Size of testing set used
Performance (binomial classification)	Main criterion (accuracy, precision, recall, F-measure)	This operator is used for statistical performance evaluation of binominal classification tasks

dataset" after every complete rotation of obtaining performance metrics until all the three datasets have been passed through the model.

In order to successfully carry out the training and testing process, some parameters are used to achieve the best result. These parameters are defined in Table 5.1.

K nearest neighbor algorithm has been studied for different number of neighbors. The output result is shown in Table 5.2. A key point in this filter is growth in fault occurrence according to increase in the number of Neighbors. The presented results show that, since the number of samples in each class is not balanced, decrease in the number of Neighbors may improve the result. In addition, Table 5.3 shows the resulting

Table 5.2 Output Result of Different Number of Neighbors

	K-NN using 10 x-Validation						
Metrics	**K-NN1**	**K-NN2**	**K-NN3**	**K-NN4**	**K-NN5**	**K-NN6**	**K-NN7**
Accuracy	99.37%	*99.16%*	99.20%	98.69%	98.57%	95. 86%	98.97%
Precision	99.76%	99.76%	99.43%	99.43%	99.27%	99.67%	*99.59%*
Recall	99.35%	99.18%	99.43%	98.69%	98.69%	98.69%	98.94%
F Score	99.55%	99.47%	99.43%	99.06%	98.98%	99.18%	99.26%

Table 5.3 Confusion Matrix Resulted from *K* Nearest Neighbor

	K = 1		*K* = 2		*K* = 3	
Real Classes	**Phishing**	**Non-phishing**	**Phishing**	**Non-phishing**	**Phishing**	**Non-phishing**
Phishing	99.43%	0.22%	99.43%	1.92%	98.67%	1.33%
Non-phishing	0.55%	*9935%*	0.55%	99.18%	1.28%	99.43%

```
Generating stratified folds:
// Data structure with a list for each convolution of a
// Class.
List [] [] folds: = new List [| C |] [k];
for each class c do
        int counter = 0;
        for each object o in C do
                folds [c] [counter mod k]. insert (o)
                counter = counter +1
        enddo
enddo
```

Fig. 5.3. Pseudocode for Stratified sampling type.

confusion matrix from K Nearest Neighbor which is then used to select the closest Nearest Neighbor. K-NN1 shows the best result. Therefore, K-NN1 is used in the implementation shown in further section.

Another key parameter used in training and testing process is the "sampling type." In this implementation, stratified sampling was chosen because the variable type of the dataset used is set to binomial. Figure 5.3 shows the pseudocode for stratified sampling type.

During implementation of this phase, different parameters have been used to train and test the classifiers in order to justify the parameters used. A major parameter alternated several times during the initial process is the number of validations used as described in Figure 5.1.

Meanwhile, after using nine different validation number from 10 to 90 such that $x = [10, 20, 30, .., 90]$ and the standard deviation of the results examined, it was concluded that because of the insignificance of the standard deviation value, any of the results can be used. Tables 5.4–5.7 shows the accuracy, precision, recall, and f-measure respectively, of the reference classifiers showing the average and standard deviation of all the nine validation number used whereas Figures 5.4–5.7 show the plot of average against standard deviation of accuracy, precision, recall, and f-measure, respectively.

Looking at the accuracy of K-NN1 and K-NN2 shown in Table 5.4, it is obvious to conclude that K-NN1 performs better than K-NN2 and as such K-NN1 is chosen over K-NN2 in the further implementation phases discussed later on in this chapter. Based on the justification discussed for number of validation, each of the reference algorithms was

Table 5.4 Accuracy Results for Validation Numbers Used Respectively

CV	C4.5	LR	K-NN1	K-NN2	SVM
10	99.09%	99.03%	99.37%	99.26%	99.03%
20	99.08%	99.03%	99.37%	99.26%	97.88%
30	98.97%	99.03%	99.37%	99.26%	99.03%
40	98.97%	99.03%	99.37%	99.26%	99.03%
50	99.03%	99.03%	99.37%	99.26%	99.03%
60	98.98%	99.03%	99.37%	99.26%	98.80%
70	99.09%	99.03%	99.37%	99.26%	98.63%
80	98.97%	99.03%	99.43%	99.32%	99.03%
90	99.03%	99.03%	99.37%	99.25%	98.62%
AVG	**99.02%**	**99.03%**	**99.38%**	**99.27%**	**98.79%**
STD	**0.0005011**	**2.2204E-16**	**0.00018856**	**0.000195**	**0.00360648**

trained and tested across the three sets of dataset and the resulting output of this process is shown in Tables 5.8–5.11. Corresponding charts of the result obtained are shown in Figures 5.8–5.11.

Scrutinizing the results obtained from individual classifier performance across the varying dataset used, it was observed that K-NN perform best with Set A based on accuracy and f-measure. Perhaps,

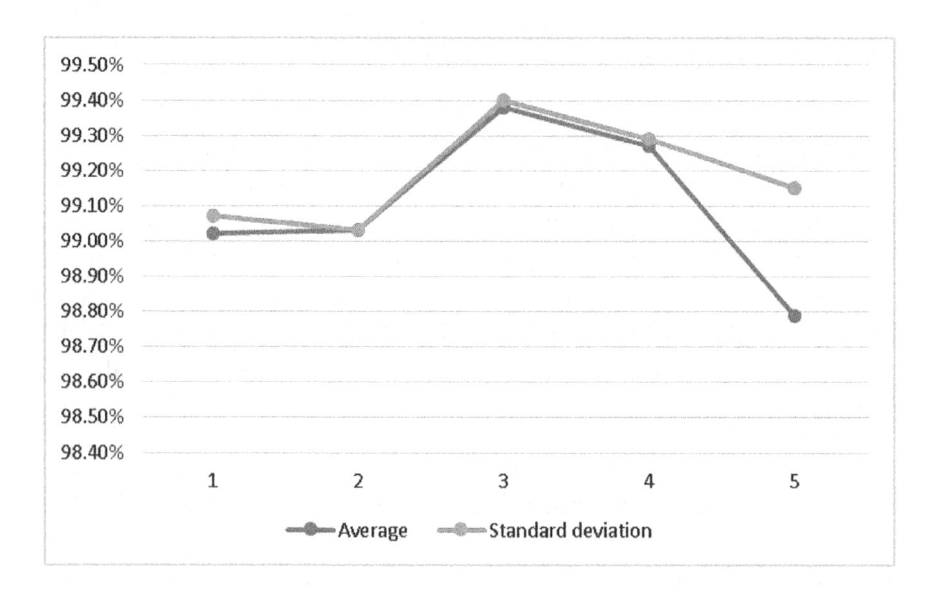

Fig. 5.4. Overall average and standard deviation for accuracy.

Table 5.5 Precision Results for Validation Numbers Used Respectively

CV	C4.5	LR	K-NN1	K-NN2	SYM
10	99.75%	99.92%	99.76%	99.76%	99.92%
20	99.76%	99.92%	99.76%	99.76%	99.83%
30	99.68%	99.92%	99.76%	99.76%	99.92%
40	99.68%	99.92%	99.76%	99.76%	99.92%
50	99.76%	99.92%	99.76%	99.76%	99.92%
60	99.68%	99.92%	99.76%	99.76%	99.92%
70	99.92%	99.52%	99.76%	99.76%	99.92%
80	99.77%	99.92%	99.77%	99.77%	99.92%
90	99.77%	99.93%	99.77%	99.77%	99.93%
AVG	99. 75%	99.88%	99. 76%	99. 76%	99.91%
STD	0.00070361	0.00126139	4.1S74E-05	4.15-T4E-05	0.00028846

considering both precision and recall may give a confusing interpretation to the results without considering the f-measure which is the harmonic mean of combined precision and recall. Therefore, investigating the f-measure of individual classifiers across varying dataset as shown in Table 5.11, it is obvious that K-NN f-measure is the highest at 99.55%. Hence, the best performed classifier out of all the reference classifiers is chosen as K-NN (Table 5.12).

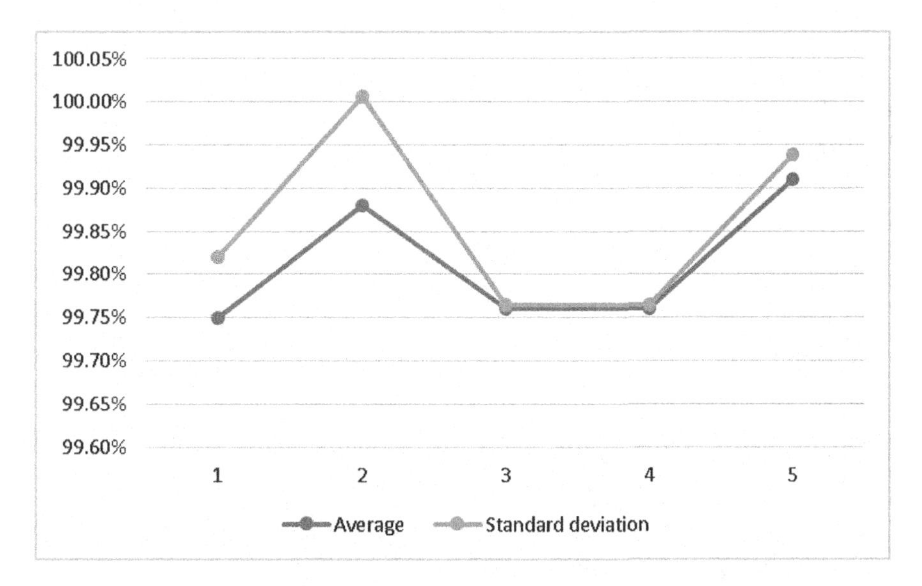

Fig. 5.5. Overall average and standard deviation for precision.

Table 5.6 Recall Results for Validation Numbers Used Respectively

CV	C4.5	LR	K-NN 1	K-NN 2	SVM
10	98.94%	98.69%	99.35%	99.18%	98.69%
20	98.94%	98.70%	99.35%	99.18%	97.14%
30	98.85%	98.69%	99.35%	99.18%	98.69%
40	98.86%	98.70%	99.35%	99.19%	98.70%
50	98.86%	98.69%	99.35%	99.19%	98.69%
60	98.87%	98.70%	99.36%	99.19%	98.38%
70	98.76%	98.67%	99.33%	99.17%	98.08%
80	98.77%	98.69%	99.43%	99.27%	98.69%
90	98.85%	98.68%	99.34%	99.18%	98.08%
AVG	98.86%	98.69%	99.36%	99.19%	98.35%
STD	0.0005871	9.4281E-05	0.0002708	0.00028197	0.00493929

It can be observed in Table 5.13 that the false alarm rate of K-NN is substantially small and as such considered a good classifier since the output result shows that the algorithm correctly classified most of the instances and a false negative of 0.800 is the resulting error rate obtained.

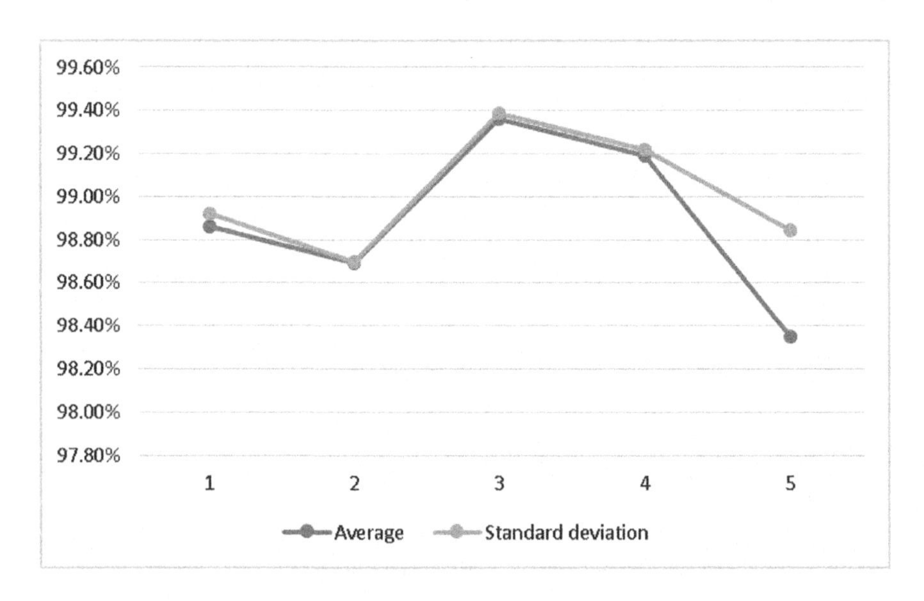

Fig. 5.6. Overall average and standard deviation for recall.

Table 5.7 F-Measure Results for Validation Numbers Used Respectively					
CV	C4.5	LR	K-NN1	K-NN2	SVM
10	99.34%	99.30%	99.55%	99.47%	99.30%
20	99.34%	99.30%	99.55%	99.47%	98.32%
30	99.25%	99.30%	99.55%	99.46%	99.30%
40	99.26%	99.29%	99.55%	99.46%	99.29%
50	99.30%	99.29%	99.55%	99.47%	99.29%
60	99.25%	99.29%	99.55%	99.46%	99.12%
70	99.31%	99.30%	99.53%	99.45%	98.90%
80	99.24%	99.28%	99.58%	99.50%	99.28%
90	99.28%	99.28%	99.54%	99.47%	98.87%
AVG	99.29%	99.29%	99.55%	99.47%	99.07%
STD	0.00036549	7.8567E-05	0.00012472	0.00013147	0.00312769

Figure 5.12 shows the ROC curve for K-NN. This shows the plot of true positive rate and false positive rate in order to provide a principled mechanism to explore operating point tradeoffs. The ROC obtained is 0.500.

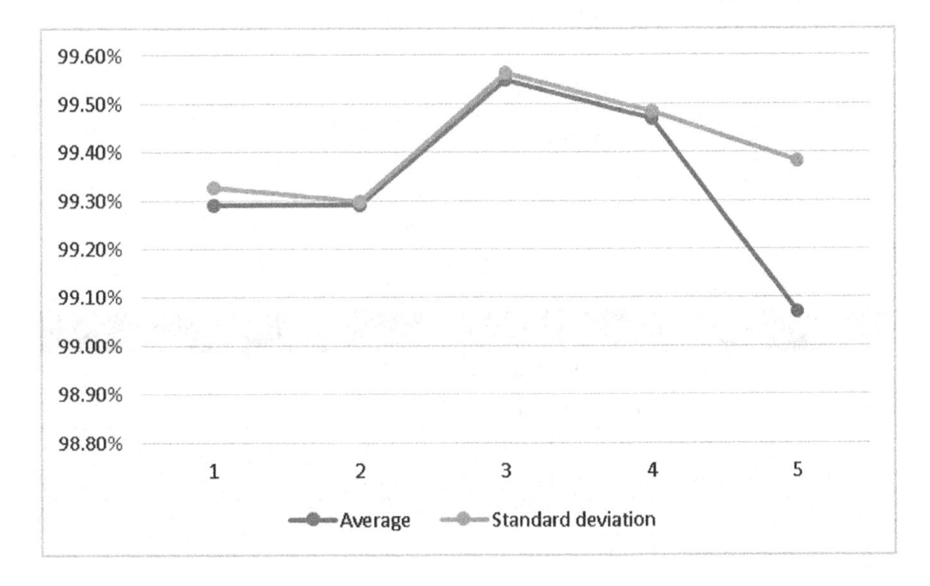

Fig. 5.7. Overall average and standard deviation for F-measure.

Table 5.8 Accuracy of Individual Classifier in Varying Dataset

Individual Technique Accuracy				
SET	**C4.5**	**LR**	**KNN**	**SVM**
A	99.14%	99.03%	**99.37%**	99.03%
B	99.31%	99.31%	99.31%	99.31%
C	99.26%	99.26%	98.80%	99.26%

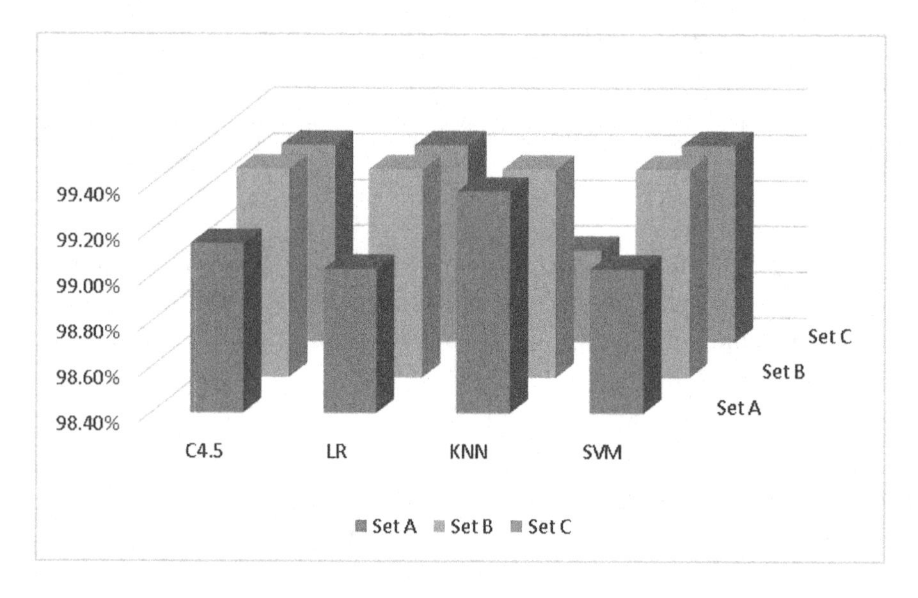

Fig. 5.8. Plot of accuracy across varying dataset.

Table 5.9 Precision of Individual Classifier in Varying Dataset

Individual Technique Precision				
SET	**C4.5**	**LR**	**KNN**	**SVM**
A	99.92%	99.92%	99.76%	99.92%
B	99.88%	99.88%	99.66%	99.88%
C	98.51%	98.51%	98.66%	98.51%

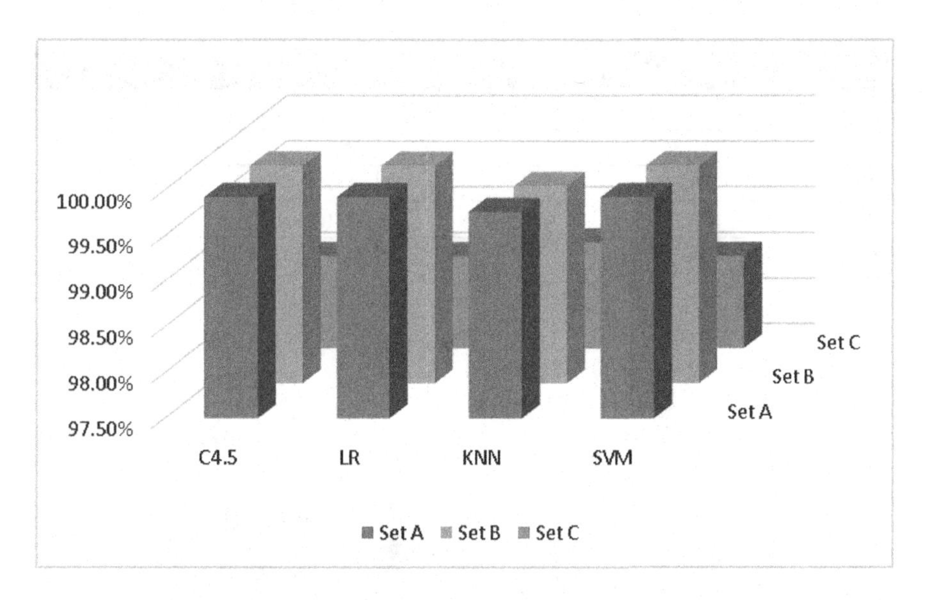

Fig. 5.9. Plot of precision across varying dataset.

Table 5.10 Recall of Individual Classifier in Varying Dataset

Individual Technique Recal				
SET	**C4.5**	**LR**	**KNN**	**SVM**
A	98.86%	98.69%	99.35%	98.69%
B	98.74%	98.74%	98.97%	98.74%
C	99.05%	99.05%	97.34%	99.05%

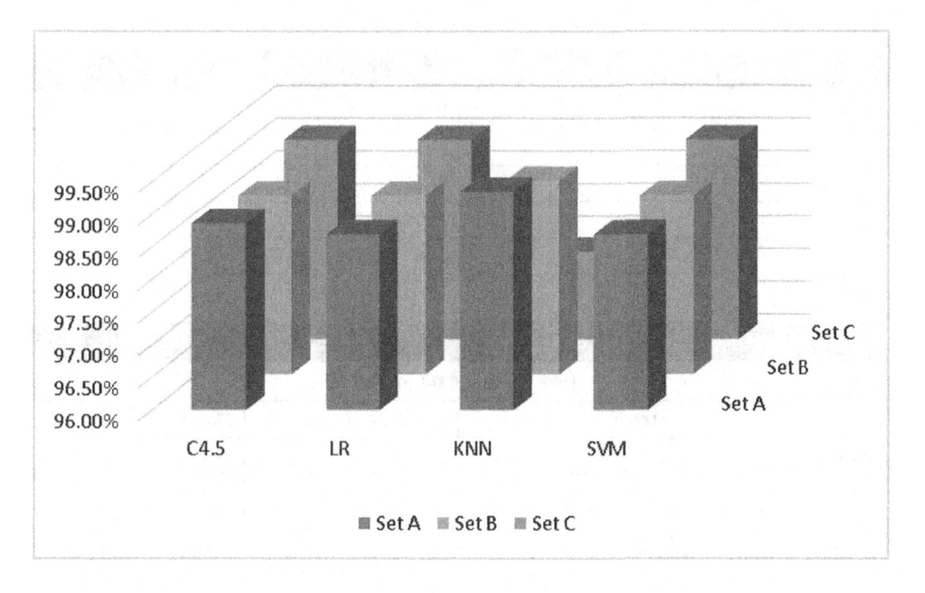

Fig. 5.10. Plot of recall across varying dataset.

Table 5.11 F-Score of Individual Classifier in Varying Dataset

Individual Technique F-score				
SET	**C4.5**	**LR**	**KNN**	**SVM**
A	99.38%	99.30%	**99.55%**	99.30%
B	99.31%	99.31%	99.31%	99.31%
C	98.76%	98.76%	97.98%	99.31%

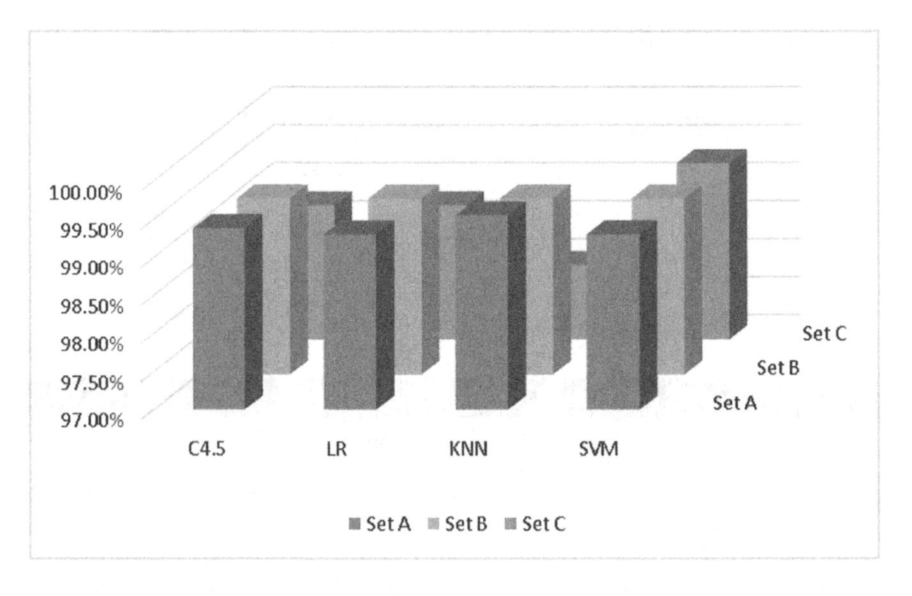

Fig. 5.11. Plot of f-measure across varying dataset.

Table 5.12 Best Performed Individual Classifier

SET A	**K-NN**
Accuracy	99.37%
Precision	99.76%
Recall	99.35%
F Score	99.55%

Table 5.13 False Alarm Rate of K-NN

False Negative: 0.800 +/− 0.600			
	True 1	**True 0**	**Class Precision**
Pred. 1	522	8	98.49%
Pred. 0	3	1217	99.75%
Class recall	99.43%	99.35%	

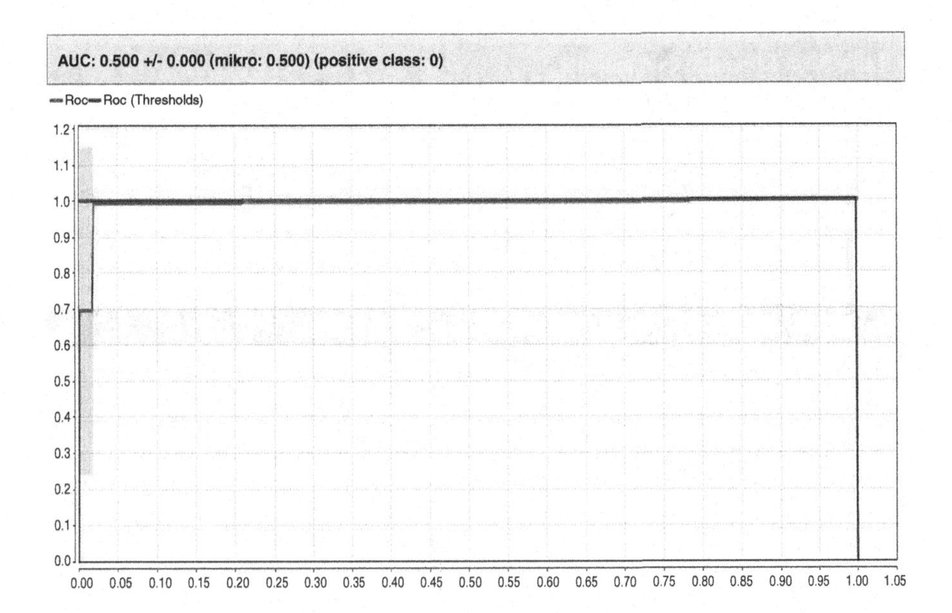

Fig. 5.12. ROC curve for K-NN.

5.4 ENSEMBLE DESIGN AND VOTING SCHEME

Experiments using varying dataset was conducted in Section 5.3 and based on the output of this conduct, the committee of ensemble was designed. The ensemble algorithm chosen was the simple majority voting algorithm, for this reason an odd number of constituent classifiers was required. From the pool of four classifiers, all sets of classifiers of size three were chosen for ensembles. This meant that there were a total of four classifier ensembles. The components of these are summarized in Table 5.14. These ensembles were evaluated using the same metrics as the individual techniques in Section 5.3. Tables 5.15–5.17 show the results obtained for the four ensembles which are further illustrated in the charts shown in Figures 5.13–5.15. These results are compared to those in Section 5.3 and presented in a later section.

Based on the result obtained from ensemble, it becomes obvious that all the ensembles performed equally in Set B and also the results obtained are the best of the three datasets. Also, this testifies that all the ensembles perform best when the dataset is equally divided between phishing and non-phishing. Since all the ensembles have the same result when Set B dataset is used then it can be concluded that any of these

Table 5.14 Ensemble Components

Ensemble	Algl	Alg2	Alg3
Ensemble 1	KNN	C4.5	LR
Ensemble 2	KNN	C4.5	SVM
Ensemble 3	KNN	LR	SVM
Ensemble 4	C4.5	LR	SVM

Table 5.15 Ensemble Result Using the SET A

SET A	ENS1	ENS2	ENS3	ENS4
Accuracy	99.20%	99.20%	99.03%	99.03%
Precision	99.92%	99.92%	99.92%	99.92%
Recall	98.94%	98.94%	98.69%	98.69%
F Score	99.42%	99.42%	99.30%	99.30%

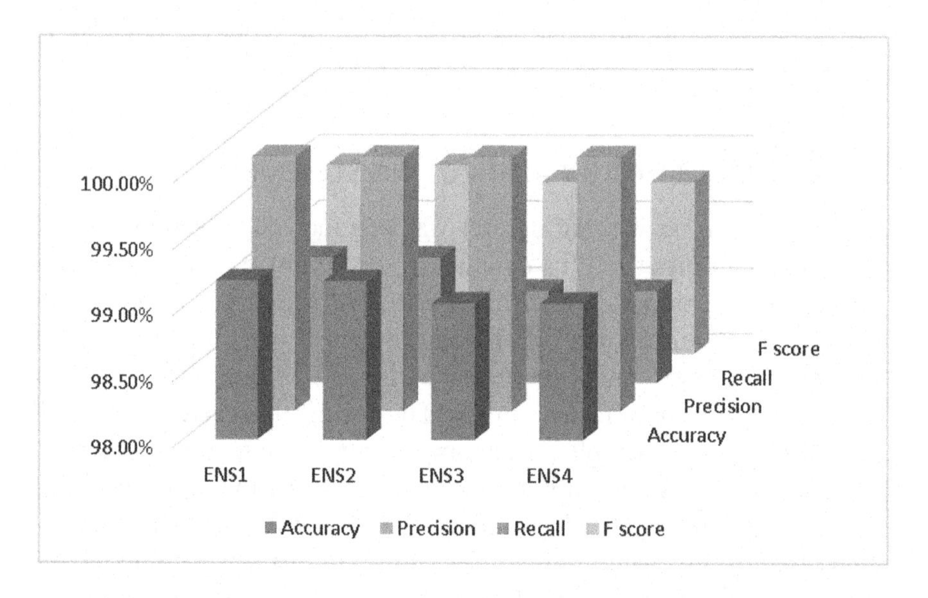

Fig. 5.13. Plot of performance metric and ensembles across SET A.

Table 5.16 Ensemble Result Using the SET B Dataset

SET B	ENS1	ENS2	ENS3	ENS4
Accuracy	99.31%	99.31%	99.31%	99.31%
Precision	99.88%	99.88%	99.88%	99.88%
Recall	98.74%	98.74%	98.74%	98.74%
F Score	99.31%	99.31%	99.31%	99.31%

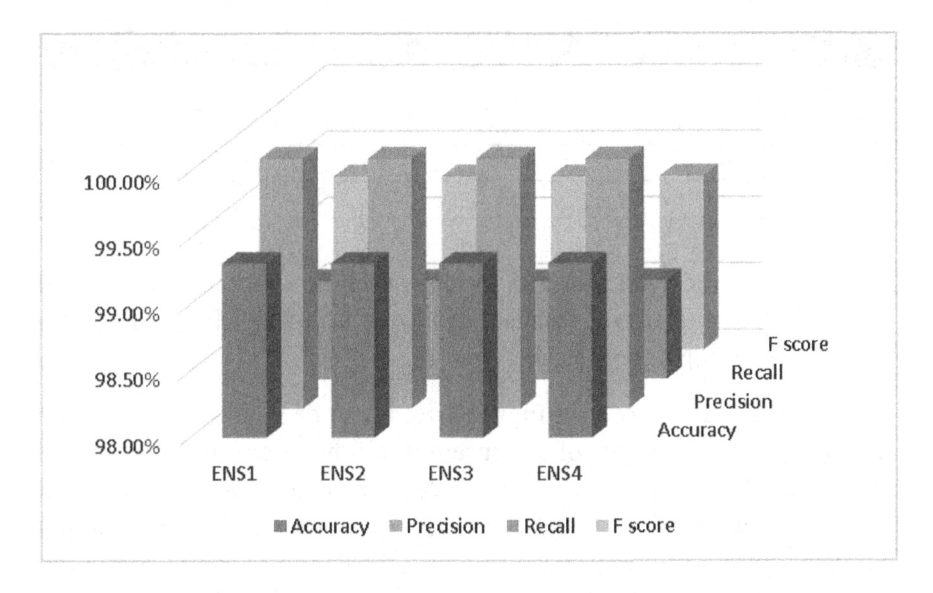

Fig. 5.14. Plot of performance metric and ensembles across SET B.

Table 5.17 Ensemble Result Using the SET C Dataset

SET C	ENS1	ENS2	ENS3	ENS4
Accuracy	99.26%	99.26%	99.26%	99.26%
Precision	98.51%	98.51%	98.51%	98.51%
Recall	99.05%	99.05%	99.05%	99.05%
F Score	98.76%	98.76%	98.76%	98.76%

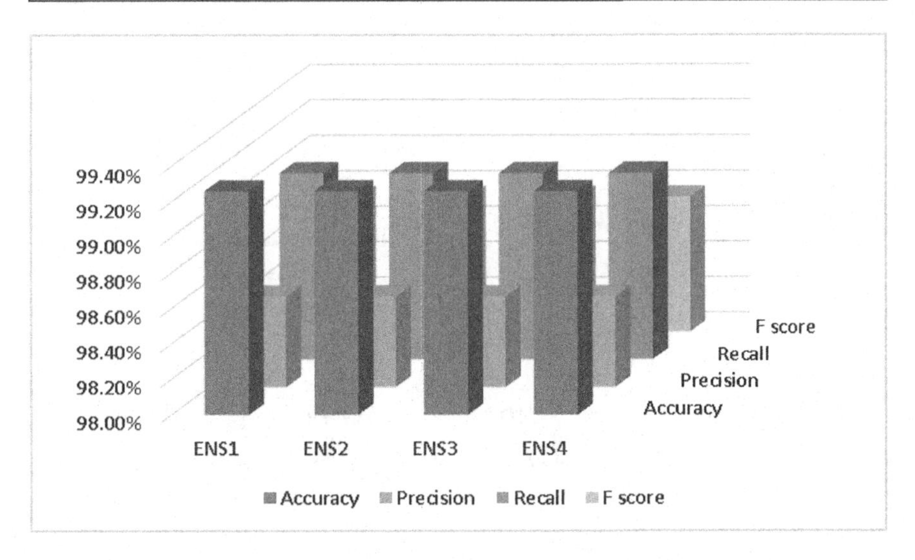

Fig. 5.15. Plot of performance metric and ensembles across SET C.

Table 5.18 Accuracy of Individual Ensemble Across Varying Dataset

Dataset	ENS1	ENS2	ENS3	ENS4
SET A	99.20%	99.20%	99.03%	99 03%
SET B	99.31%	99.31%	99.31%	99.31%
SET C	99.26%	99.26%	99.26%	99.26%

ensembles can be used. Table 5.18 shows the accuracy obtained from the ensembles with varying dataset. A plot of accuracy of the ensembles across the varying dataset is shown in Figure 5.15.

From the graph shown in Figure 5.16, it can be seen that in both Set B and Set C, the accuracy of the ensembles is the same and in Set A, the last two ensembles (ENS3 and ENS4) diverged in accuracy as compared to the first two ensembles (ENS1 and ENS2). This sudden drop in accuracy is due to the weak performance of LR and SVM as compared to C4.5 and K-NN as discussed in the previous section. Meanwhile, the results obtained from ensemble using Set B shows the same value for all the ensembles and as such, any of the ensembles in Set B can be selected as the best performed ensemble. ENS1 is selected and Table 5.19 shows the values obtained from this ensemble whereas Table 5.20 shows the false alarm rate of the ensemble classifier.

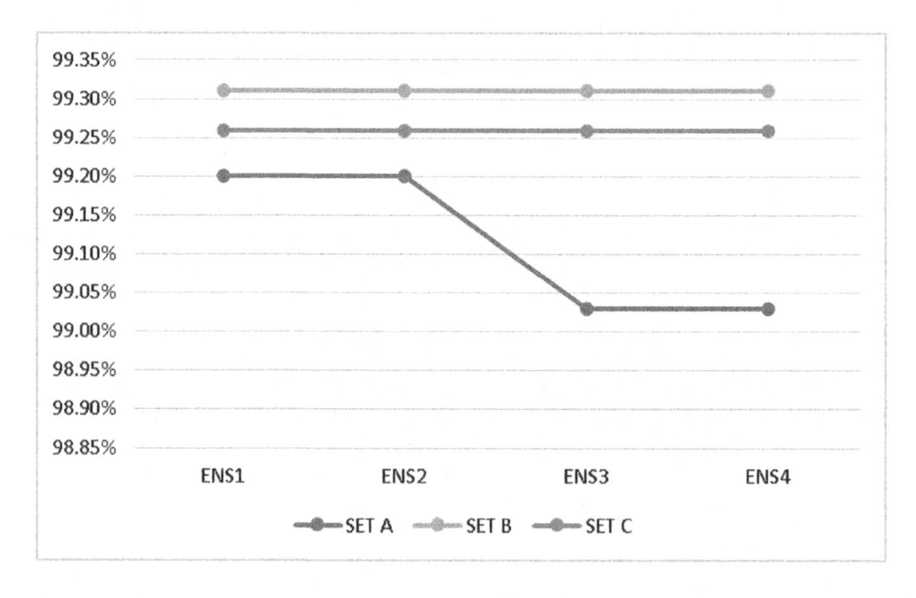

Fig. 5.16. Plot of accuracy of the ensembles across the varying dataset.

Table 5.19 Selected Ensemble Classifier

SET B	ENS1
Accuracy	99.31%
Precision	99.88%
Recall	98.74%
F Score	99.31%

Table 5.20 False Alarm Rate of ENS1

False Negative : 1.100+/− 1.136			
	True 1	True 0	Class Precision
Pred. 1	874	11	98.76%
Pred. 0	1	864	99.88%
Class recall	99.89%	98.74%	

The false alarm rate of ENS1 as shown in Table 5.20 indicates that most of the predictions were classified correctly and a few were classified wrongly. Considering the margin of error as obtained from the false alarm value of 1.10, it can be concluded that this ensemble is very accurate in its classification. The results shown in Table 5.19 are used for comparison in the next phase of this project that is discussed in the next section. Also, it is indicated that the ROC of 0.697 is achieved as shown in Figure 5.17.

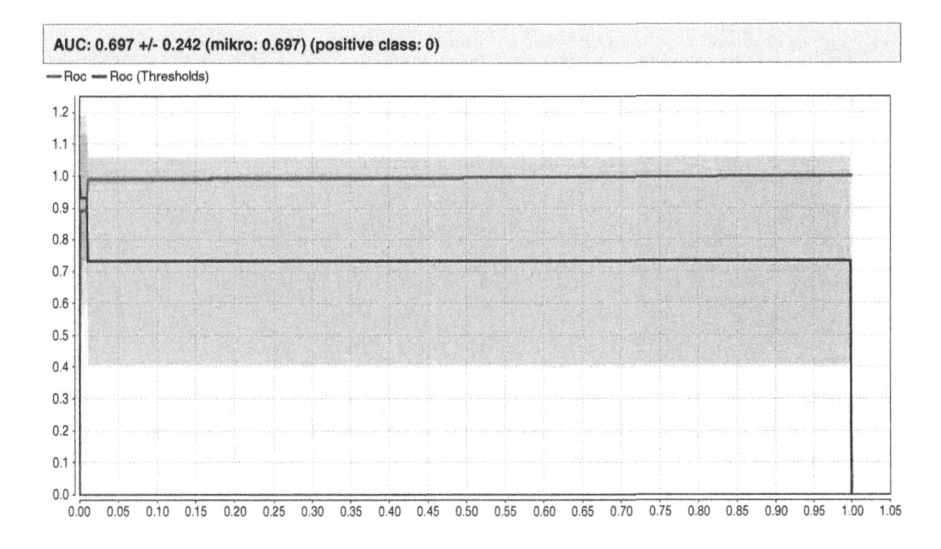

Fig. 5.17. ROC of the best performed ensemble classifier.

5.5 COMPARATIVE STUDY

This section recaps the objective three of the research framework discussed in Chapter 3. A comparative study between the best performed individual classifier and the best performed ensemble is discussed in this section. Table 5.21 shows the results of both the best performed individual algorithm and ensemble algorithm. Also, Figure 5.18 shows the plot of the two best performed algorithms in individual and ensemble methods, respectively.

Figure 5.16 shows the trend of the different performance metrics across K-NN and ENS1 algorithm. It can be observed that even though the best individual algorithm performs slightly better in accuracy than the best ensemble algorithm, the precision of ENS1 is higher than

Table 5.21 Resulting Best Individual and Ensemble Algorithm

Metrics	K-NN	ENS1
Accuracy	99.37%	99.31%
Precision	99.76%	99.88%
Recall	99.35%	98.74%
F Score	99.55%	99.31%

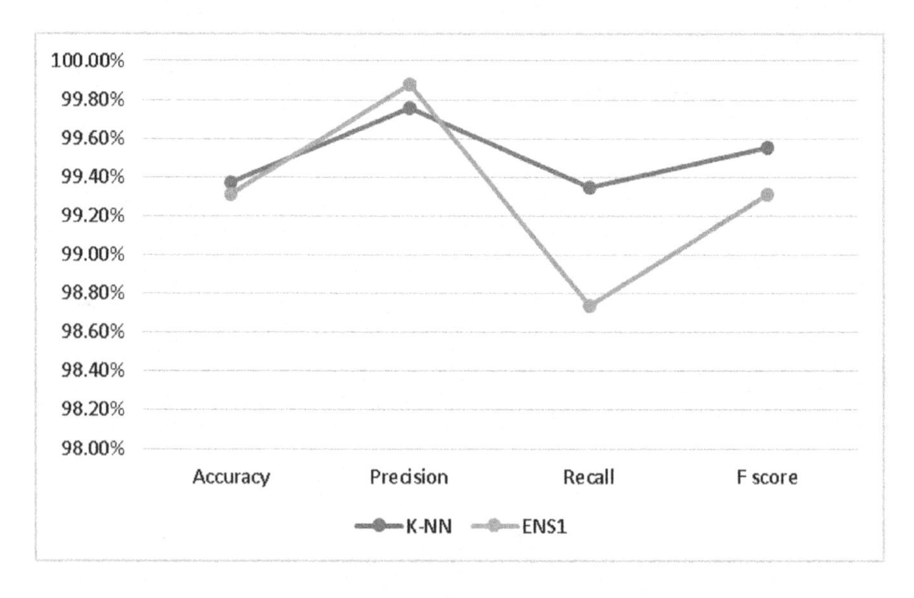

Fig. 5.18. Plot of best individual against best ensemble algorithm.

K-NN and this can be used to conclude that ensemble can be used to improve the performance of individual base algorithms. However, the performance of ensemble classifiers can decrease across more ensemble component classifiers if introduced to classifiers with very low performance as compared to the rest. This can be ensured by checking the accuracy of the base classifiers and the error rate must be checked to ensure varying error rates.

5.6 SUMMARY

This chapter presents the implementation and results of Phase 2 and Phase 3 of the research methodology to investigate the more suitable method for increasing detection rate and in determining the best composition of classifiers that can give a good detection rate of phishing websites. Individual classifiers, namely, C4.5, LR, K-NN, and SVM were trained and tested with the reference performance metrics, namely, accuracy, precision, recall, and f-measure. The resulting best performed classifier scored 99.37% and 0.800 on false alarm rate. This chapter also provides the algorithms used in design ensemble that are the same with the algorithms used in individual classifier technique. This committee of ensembles was synergized through majority voting. The proposed ensemble design scored 99.31% on the overall accuracy and 1.10 on false alarm rate. The problem of high false alarm rate has been partially addressed. Results from the validation tests give evidence that the overall performance of the chosen ensemble classifier is almost the same as that of the best individual classifier model. The next chapter provides the conclusion of the study.

CHAPTER 6
Conclusions

6.1 CONCLUDING REMARKS

The importance to safeguard online users from becoming victims of online fraud, divulging confidential information to an attacker among other effective uses of phishing as an attacker's tool, phishing detection tools play a vital role in ensuring a secure online experience for users. Unfortunately, many of the existing phishing-detection tools, especially those that depend on an existing blacklist, suffer limitations such as low detection accuracy and high false alarm that is often caused by either a delay in blacklist update as a result of human verification process involved in classification or perhaps, it can be attributed to human error in classification which may lead to improper classification of the classes. These critical issues have drawn many researchers to work on various approaches to improve detection accuracy of phishing attacks and to minimize false alarm rate. The inconsistent nature of attacks behaviors and continuously changing URL phish patterns require timely updating of the reference model. Therefore, it requires an effective technique to regulate retraining as to enable machine learning algorithm to actively adapt to the changes in phish patterns.

This study focus on investigating a better detection approach and to design an ensemble of classifier suitable to be used in phishing detection. Figure 6.1 summarizes the design and implementation phases leading to the proposed better detection model.

Phase 1 focuses on dataset gathering, preprocessing, and feature extraction. The objective is to process data for use in Phase 2. The gathering stage is done manually by using Google crawler and Phishtank, each of this data gathering methods were tested to ensure a valid output. The dataset is validated first after gathering, then normalized, features extraction and finally dataset division. Nine features were selected for this project to ensure an optimum result from the classifiers and also,

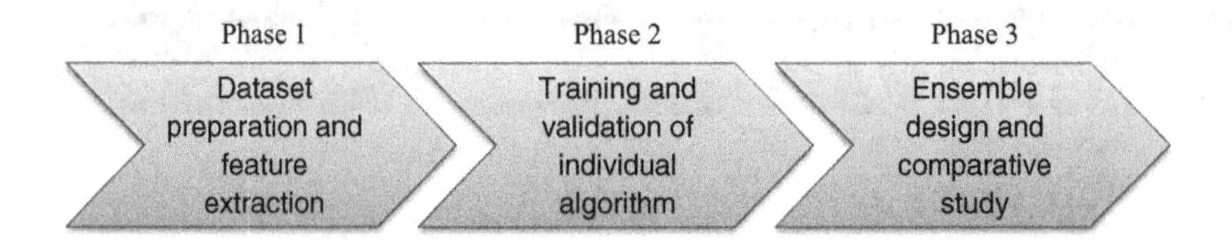

Fig. 6.1. Design and development phases leading to the proposed model.

since using a small feature set will invariably speed up processing time for training and for classification of new instances. These features were selected on the basis of the weighted performance of each feature by using information gain algorithm to ensure that only the best features were selected. This phase focuses on ensuring that the dataset preprocessing is done appropriately to accommodate the models selected.

Phase 2 focuses on design and implementation of training and validating model using single classifier. A predefined performance metrics is used as a measurement of accuracy, precision, recall, and f-measure. The objective of this phase is to test the performance of individual classifiers in the pool of varying dataset as divided in Chapter 4 and select the most performed of all the reference classifiers. An accuracy of 99.37% was obtained from K-NN which is the highest as compared to other classifiers referenced. Although it was also observed that some of the classifiers like K-NN and C4.5 maintained a close range performance, same cannot be said of the remaining two classifiers that appeared lacking behind in performance. The performance of K-NN is not surprising since the dataset used is of a small set and as such K-NN often perform better with small dataset but the performance decreases has the size of the dataset increases (Kim and Huh, 2011). Also, since the performance of KNN is primarily determined by the choice of K, the best K was found by varying it from 1 to 7; and found that KNN performs best when K = 1. This as well, helped in the high accuracy of KNN compared to other classifiers used.

Phase 3 which corresponds to the third objective is divided into two parts, one is the ensemble design and the other is the comparative study between the best ensemble and the best individual classifier that was selected in Phase 2. To design a good ensemble, only three algorithms are used for individual ensemble due to the selection of majority voting as the ensemble algorithm, odd number of algorithms must be used to select the committee of ensembles. For every instance of each ensemble, an ensemble design of three algorithms is being selected until all the algorithms have been combined evenly. The design ensemble performed very well with an accuracy of 99.31% for the best-performed ensemble and this result is then compared with that obtained in Phase 2. The outcome of the comparison suggests that if K-NN algorithm is removed or if the size of the dataset is increased, the ensemble will most likely perform better than the individual algorithm. This investigation will be considered as part of future work.

6.2 RESEARCH CONTRIBUTION

This section gives a list of contributions as outcomes to this research. The following subsections discussed the major contributions to this research.

6.2.1 Dataset Preprocessing Technique

Since the dataset used in this project is manually collected for non-phishing and then phishing URLs is extracted from Phishtank repository, the remaining part of preprocessing the data and extracting the features were carried out as part of the objectives of this project. During preprocessing, it was ensured that all the dataset involved are tested and confirmed alive as it is known that phishing websites are often uploaded for a limited time and most of them go offline after a couple of days. The essence of this is to ensure that no bogus result is being presented and as such the results collected from the implementation phase are very accurate. One of the major problems observed in other similar research is that there is no assurance that the dataset collected from most of the phishing and non-phishing repository have been tested alive or not and as such the results may be subjected to glitches of error.

6.2.2 Validation Technique

The dataset is validated with individual algorithms nine times to ensure that the right pattern of validation is selected. This cross-validations are set to [10, 20, 30… 90] after which the results based on the performance metrics were averaged and the standard deviation calculated to ensure the deviation limit of the result to justify the cross validation used. In most of the related researches, validation is often set to a range of [5, 10, 15] but in order to ensure the performance of this algorithms and better prove beyond doubts that the cross-validation used is the most efficient. Although it turns out that any of the cross-validation tested can be used since the deviation margin of the results is negligible, the importance of certainty cannot be over emphasized.

6.2.3 Design Ensemble Method

In most research, especially the ones involved with majority voting, often times the number of algorithms used is four and a decision is taken to remove the least-performed classifier but in the case of this project, the last two algorithms performed almost the same and as such the chance of removing one of them without being biased is uncertain. Because of this reason, each algorithm is marched with other algorithm in a committee of three which leads us to having four ensembles. Therefore, the problem of selecting one of two closely performed classifiers has been resolved.

6.3 RESEARCH IMPLICATION

Most of the studies have been focused on phishing detection using preprocessed data. It is obvious that when a selected set of features are extracted during preprocessing, it is easier to develop a dataset that is entirely suitable for phishing. This has been carried out in Chapter 4 to ensure that each of the features selected has been scrutinized on the basis of weight impact. Hence, a more satisfactory classification rate is achieved.

6.4 RECOMMENDATIONS FOR FUTURE RESEARCH

This research uncovers new possible areas for further research as the following:

1. For future work, other types of voting implementation could be employed in order to find the most efficient of them.
2. Using a dataset with a wider range of variation can be used to improve the performance of c4.5 and SVM as they both perform better with an increase in dataset size.
3. Other features should be alternated with the current features and also the impact of increasing features can be studied to better

understand the threshold of the classifiers in correctly classifying dataset with varying feature selection.

6.5 CLOSING NOTE

This book addresses the research problem comprehensively through synergy of different machine learning algorithms both individually and in-design ensemble training and validation. The issue of low detection rate has been addressed through selective feature extraction, well-performed machine learning algorithm and an unbiased committee of ensemble. This has also efficiently resolved the problem of high false alarm during classification. Finally, composition committee of ensemble has been designed efficiently without being biased. This is achieved by designing an ensemble in which all the reference algorithms participated in. In addition, this research has opened up new research opportunities with respect to the enhancement of the ensemble model by testing new ensemble methods to ensure the best possible ensemble of classifier is used.

REFERENCES

A.-P.W.G., 2010. Global phishing survey: domain name use and trends in 2h2010.

Abbasi, A., Chen, H., 2007. Detecting fake escrow websites using rich fraud cues and kernel based methods. Proceedings of the 17th Workshop on Information Technologies and Systems, 55–60.

Abbasi, A., Chen, H., 2009a. A comparison of fraud cues and classification methods for fake escrow website detection. Inform. Technol. Manage. 10, 83–101.

Abbasi, A., Chen, H., 2009b. A comparison of tools for detecting fake websites. Computer 42, 78–86.

Abbasi, A., Zahedi, F.M., Kaza, S., 2012. Detecting fake medical websites using recursive trust labeling. ACM Trans. Inform. Syst. 30 (4), 22.

Abbasi, A., Zhang, Z., Zimbra, D., Chen, H., Nunamaker Jr, J.F., 2010. Detecting fake websites: the contribution of statistical learning theory. MIS quart. 34, 435.

Aburrous, M., Hossain, M.A., Thabatah, F. Dahal, K. Intelligent phishing website detection system using fuzzy techniques. Information and Communication Technologies: From Theory to Applications, 2008. ICTTA 2008. 3rd International Conference on, 2008. IEEE, 1–6.

Afroz, S., Greenstadt, R., 2009. Phishzoo: an automated web phishing detection approach based on profiling and fuzzy matching. Technical Report DU-CS-09-03, Drexel University.

Afroz, S. Greenstadt, R., 2011. Phishzoo: detecting phishing websites by looking at them. Semantic Computing (ICSC), 2011 Fifth IEEE International Conference on, 2011. IEEE, 368–375.

Airoldi, E., Malin, B., 2004. Data mining challenges for electronic safety: the case of fraudulent intent detection in e-mails. Proceedings of the workshop on privacy and security aspects of data mining, 57–66.

Akthar, F., Hahne, C., 2012. RapidMiner 5: Operator Reference. Rapid-I GmbH.

Al Shalabi, L. Shaaban, Z., 2006. Normalization as a preprocessing engine for data mining and the approach of preference matrix. Dependability of Computer Systems, 2006. DepCos-RELCOMEX'06. International Conference on, 2006. IEEE, 207–214.

Alnajim, A., Munro, M., 2009. An Approach to the Implementation of the Anti-Phishing Tool for Phishing Websites Detection. Intelligent Networking and Collaborative Systems, 2009. INCOS'09. International Conference on, 2009. IEEE, 105–112.

Anewalt, K., Ackermann, E., 2005. Open source, freeware, and shareware resources for web programming: tutorial presentation. J. Comput. Sci. CollegeV 20, 198–200.

Atighetchi, M., Pal, P., 2009. Attribute-based prevention of phishing attacks. Network Computing and Applications, 2009. NCA 2009. Eighth IEEE International Symposium on, 2009. IEEE, 266–269.

Basnet, R., Mukkamala, S., Sung, A., 2008. Detection of phishing attacks: a machine learning approach. Soft Comput. Appl. Indust., 373–383.

Basnet, R.B., Sung, A.H., Liu, Q., 2011. Rule-Based Phishing Attack Detection. International Conference on Security and Management (SAM 2011). Las Vegas, NV.

Berend, D., Paroush, J., 1998. When is Condorcet's Jury Theorem valid? Soc. Choice Welfare 15, 481–488.

Chen, J., Guo, C., 2006. Online detection and prevention of phishing attacks. Communications and Networking in China, 2006. ChinaCom'06. First International Conference on, 2006. IEEE, 1–7.

Chen, K.T., Chen, J.Y., Huang, C.R., Chen, C.S., 2009. Fighting phishing with discriminative keypoint features. IEEE Internet Computing 13, 56–63.

Chou, N., Ledesma, R., Teraguchi, Y., Boneh, D., Mitchell, J.C., 2004. Client-side defense against web-based identity theft. 11th Annual Network and Distributed System Security Symposium (NDSS'04), San Diego, USA.

Chua, C.E.H, Wareham, J., 2004. Fighting internet auction fraud: an assessment and proposal. Computer 37, 31–37.

Cios, K.J., Pedrycz, W., Swiniarsk, R., 1998. Data mining methods for knowledge discovery. IEEE T. Neural Networks 9, 1533–1534.

Close, T. 2009. Waterken YURL: trust management for humans (2003). Last visit on May, 30.

Dhamija, R., Tygar, J., 2005a. Phish and hips: human interactive proofs to detect phishing attacks. HIP, 69–83.

Dhamija, R., Tygar, J.D., 2005b. The battle against phishing: dynamic security skins. ACM International Conference Proceeding Series, 77–88.

Dhamija, R., Tygar, J.D., Hearst, M., 2006. Why phishing works. Proceedings of the SIGCHI conference on Human Factors in computing systems. ACM, 581–590.

Dinev, T., 2006. Why spoofing is serious internet fraud. Communications of the ACM 49, 76–82.

Dunlop, M., Groat, S., Shelly, D., 2010. GoldPhish: Using Images for Content-Based Phishing Analysis. Internet Monitoring and Protection (ICIMP), 2010 Fifth International Conference on, 2010. IEEE, 123–128.

Elkan, C., Noto, K., 2008. Learning classifiers from only positive and unlabeled data. Proceedings of the 14th ACM SIGKDD International Conference on Knowledge Discovery and Data Mining. ACM, 213–220.

Fahmy, H.M.A., Ghoneim, S.A., 2011. PhishBlock: A hybrid anti-phishing tool. Communications, Computing and Control Applications (CCCA), 2011 International Conference on, 2011. IEEE, 1–5.

Fette, I., Sadeh, N., Tomasic, A., 2007. Learning to detect phishing emails. Proceedings of the 16th international conference on World Wide Web. ACM, 649–656.

Fu, A.Y., Wenyin, L., Deng, X., 2006. Detecting phishing web pages with visual similarity assessment based on earth mover's distance (EMD). IEEE T. Depend. Secure 3, 301–311.

Gabber, E., Gibbons, P.B., Kristol, D.M., Matias, Y., Mayer, A., 1999. Consistent, yet anonymous, Web access with LPWA. Commun. ACM 42, 42–47.

Garera, S., Provos, N., Chew, M., Rubin, A.D., 2007. A framework for detection and measurement of phishing attacks. Proceedings of the 2007 ACM workshop on Recurring malcode. ACM, 1–8.

Gaurav, Madhuresh, M., Anurag, J., 2012. Anti-phishing techniques: a review. IJERA 2, 350–355.

Hall, M., Frank, E., Holmes, G., Pfahringer, B., Reutemann, P., Witten, I.H., 2009. The WEKA data mining software: an update. ACM SIGKDD Explor. Newsl. 11, 10–18.

Hariharan, P., Asgharpour, F., Camp, L.J., 2007. Nettrust – recommendation system for embedding trust in a virtual realm. Proceedings of the ACM Conference on Recommender Systems. Citeseer.

Herzberg, A., Gbara, A., 2004. Trustbar: Protecting (even naive) web users from spoofing and phishing attacks. Computer Science Department Bar Ilan University, 6.

Herzberg, A., Jbara, A., 2008. Security and identification indicators for browsers against spoofing and phishing attacks. ACM T. Internet Techn. 8, 1–36.

Huang, H., Qian, L., Wang, Y., 2012. A SVM-based technique to detect phishing URLs. Inform. Technol. J. 11, 921–925.

Jamieson, R., Wee LAND, L.P., Winchester, D., Stephens, G., Steel, A., Maurushat, A., Sarre, R., 2012. Addressing identity crime in crime management information systems: definitions, classification, and empirics. CLSR 28, 381–395.

Ji, C., Ma, S., 1997. Combinations of weak classifiers. IEEE T. Neural Networks 8, 32–42.

Jiawei, H., Kamber, M., 2001. Data Mining: Concepts and Techniques. Morgan Kaufmann, San Francisco, CA, 5.

Kim, H., Huh, J., 2011. Detecting DNS-poisoning-based phishing attacks from their network performance characteristics. Electron. Lett. 47, 656–658.

Kittler, J., Hatef, M., Duin, R.P.W., Matas, J., 1998. On combining classifiers. IEEE T. Pattern Anal. 20, 226–239.

Kristol, D. M., Gabber, E., Gibbons, P. B., Matias, Y. and Mayer, A. 1998. Design and implementation of the Lucent Personalized Web Assistant.(LPWA).

Kumaraguru, P., Rhee, Y., Acquisti, A., Cranor, L.F., Hong, J., Nunge, E., 2007. Protecting people from phishing: the design and evaluation of an embedded training email system. Proceedings of the SIGCHI conference on Human factors in computing systems. ACM, 905–914.

Lam, L., Suen, S., 1997. Application of majority voting to pattern recognition: An analysis of its behavior and performance. IEEE Trans. Syst., Man, Cybern. A, Syst., Humans 27, 553–568.

Levy, E., 2004. Criminals become tech savvy. IEEE Secur. Priv. 2, 65–68.

Li, L., Helenius, M., 2007. Usability evaluation of anti-phishing toolbars. JICV 3, 163–184.

Liu, G., Qiu, B., Wenyin, L., 2010. Automatic Detection of Phishing Target from Phishing Webpage. Pattern Recognition (ICPR), 2010 20th International Conference on, 2010. IEEE, 4153–4156.

Liu, W., Deng, X., Huang, G., Fu, A.Y., 2006. An antiphishing strategy based on visual similarity assessment. IEEE Internet Comput. 10, 58–65.

Ma, J., Saul, L.K., Savage, S., Voelker, G.M., 2009. Identifying suspicious URLs: an application of large-scale online learning. Proceedings of the 26th Annual International Conference on Machine Learning. ACM, 681–688.

Martin, A., Anutthamaa, N., Sathyavathy, M., Francois, M.M.S., Venkatesan, D.V.P., 2011. A Framework for Predicting Phishing Websites Using Neural Networks. CoRR, 1074.

Miyamoto, D., Hazeyama, H., Kadobayashi, Y., 2005. SPS: a simple filtering algorithm to thwart phishing attacks. Lect. Notes Comput. Sc, 195–209.

Miyamoto, D., Hazeyama, H., Kadobayashi, Y., 2007. A proposal of the AdaBoost-based detection of phishing sites. Proceedings of the Joint Workshop on Information Security.

Moore, T., Clayton, R., 2007. Examining the impact of website take-down on phishing. Proceedings of the anti-phishing working groups 2nd annual eCrime researchers summit. ACM, 1–13.

OpenDNS, L. L. C. PhishTank: an Anti-phishing Site.

Parker, J., 1995. Voting methods for multiple autonomous agents. Intelligent Information Systems, 1995. ANZIIS-95. Proceedings of the Third Australian and New Zealand Conference on, 1995. IEEE, 128–133.

Provos, N., Mcclain, J., Wang, K., 2006. Search worms. Proceedings of the 4th ACM workshop on Recurring malcode. ACM, 1–8.

Rahman, A., Alam, H., Fairhurst, M., 2002. Multiple classifier combination for character recognition: Revisiting the majority voting system and its variations. Lect. Notes Comput. Sc., 167–178.

Rokach, L., 2010. Ensemble-based classifiers. Artif. Intell. Rev. 33, 1–39.

Ronda, T., Saroiu, S., Wolman, A., 2008. Itrustpage: a user-assisted anti-phishing tool. ACM SIGOPS Operating Systems Review. ACM, 261–272.

Ross, B., Jackson, C., Miyake, N., Boneh, D., Mitchell, J.C., 2005. A browser plug-in solution to the unique password problem. Proceedings of the 14th Usenix Security Symposium.

RSA, 2006. Phishing special report: What we can expect for 2007? White Paper.

Ruta, D., Gabrys, B., 2000. An overview of classifier fusion methods. Comput. Inform. Syst. 7, 1–10.

Saberi, A., Vahidi, M., Bidgoli, B.M., 2007. Learn to Detect Phishing Scams Using Learning and Ensemble? Methods. Web Intelligence and Intelligent Agent Technology Workshops, 2007 IEEE/WIC/ACM International Conferences on, 2007. IEEE, 311–314.

Schneider, F., Provos, N., Moll, R., Chew, M., Rakowski, B., 2009. Phishing protection: design documentation.

See Ng, G., Singh, H., 1998. Democracy in pattern classifications: combinations of votes from various pattern classifiers. Artif. Intell. Eng. 12, 189–204.

Shreeram, V., Suban, M., Shanthi, P., Manjula, K., 2010. Anti-phishing detection of phishing attacks using genetic algorithm. Communication Control and Computing Technologies (ICCCCT), 2010 IEEE International Conference on, 2010. IEEE, 447–450.

Stajniak, A., Szostakowski, J., Skoneczny, S., 1997. Mixed neural-traditional classifier for character recognition. Advanced Imaging and Network Technologies. Int. Soc. Optics Photonics, 102–110.

Suen, C.Y., Nadal, C., Legault, R., Mai, T.A., Lam, L., 1992. Computer recognition of unconstrained handwritten numerals. IEEE Proc. 80, 1162–1180.

Todhunter, I., 1865. History of the Mathematical Theory of Probability from the time of Pascal to that of Laplace. Macmillan and Company.

Toolan, F., Carthy, J., 2009. Phishing detection using classifier ensembles. eCrime Researchers Summit, 2009. eCRIME'09., 2009. IEEE, 1–9.

Topkara, M., Kamra, A., Atallah, M., Nita-Rotaru, C., 2005. Viwid: Visible watermarking based defense against phishing. Digital Watermarking, 470–483.

Tout, H., Hafner, W., 2009. Phishpin: An identity-based anti-phishing approach. Computational Science and Engineering, 2009. CSE'09. International Conference on, 2009. IEEE, 347–352.

Whittaker, C., Ryner, B., Nazif, M., 2010. Large-scale automatic classification of phishing pages. Proc. of 17th NDSS.

Willis, P., 2009. Fake anti-virus software catches 43 million users' credit cards. Digital J.

Wu, M., Miller, R.C., Garfinkel, S.L., 2006. Do security toolbars actually prevent phishing attacks? Proceedings of the SIGCHI conference on Human Factors in computing systems. ACM, 601–610.

Xiang, G., Hong, J.I., 2009. A hybrid phish detection approach by identity discovery and keywords retrieval. Proceedings of the 18th international conference on World wide web. ACM, 571–580.

Ye, Z.E., Smith, S., Anthony, D., 2005. Trusted paths for browsers. ACM T. Inform. Syst. Secur. 8, 153–186.

Zdziarski, J., Yang, W., Judge, P., 2006. Approaches to Phishing Identification using Match and Probabilistic Digital Fingerprinting Techniques. Proc. MIT Spam Conf., 1115–1122.

Zhang, J., Ou, Y., Li, D., Xin, Y., 2012. A prior-based transfer learning method for the phishing detection. J. Networks 7, 1201–1207.

Zhang, Y., Egelman, S., Cranor, L., Hong, J., 2006. Phinding Phish: Evaluating Anti-Phishing Tools. ISOC.

Zhang, Y., Hong, J.I., Cranor, L.F., 2007. Cantina: a content-based approach to detecting phishing web sites. Proceedings of the 16th international conference on World Wide Web. ACM, 639–648.

Zhuang, W., Jiang, Q., Xiong, T., 2012. An Intelligent Anti-phishing Strategy Model for Phishing Website Detection. Distributed Computing Systems Workshops (ICDCSW), 2012 32nd International Conference on, 2012. IEEE, 51–56.

Printed in the United States
By Bookmasters